Teacherland

Teacherland

Inside the Myth of
the American Educator

Aaron Pribble

ROWMAN & LITTLEFIELD
Lanham • Boulder • New York • London

Published by Rowman & Littlefield
A wholly owned subsidiary of The Rowman & Littlefield Publishing Group, Inc.
4501 Forbes Boulevard, Suite 200, Lanham, Maryland 20706
www.rowman.com

Unit A, Whitacre Mews, 26-34 Stannary Street, London SE11 4AB

British Library Cataloguing in Publication Information Available

Library of Congress Cataloging-in-Publication Data Available

ISBN 978-1-4758-3612-7 (cloth : alk. paper)
ISBN 978-1-4758-3613-4 (pbk. : alk. paper)
ISBN 978-1-4758-3614-1 (electronic)

∞™ The paper used in this publication meets the minimum requirements of American National Standard for Information Sciences—Permanence of Paper for Printed Library Materials, ANSI/NISO Z39.48-1992.

Printed in the United States of America

For the Lunch Crew

Think and wonder, wonder and think.

—*Dr. Seuss*

Contents

Preface

Saints and Slouches

When I think about what it means to teach, I'm struck by the difference between my experience and the depiction of that experience by others. Popular perception often seems at odds with my reality. Sometimes teaching is glorified as thankless, backbreaking work and I feel as though I'm hiding a dirty secret: the job isn't really so hard or all that bad. Other times I recognize only unpleasant caricatures of the truth and feel ashamed, guilty by association.

I attribute this dissonance to educational narratives casting teachers as saints or slouches, heroes or zeros. In reality, most of us fit neither description. Yes, it's nice to know when we have made a difference, and indeed this is a primary reason many teachers enter the profession, but no, we are not saints. While doing good we also want to live well, maybe one day buy a house and drive something other than a Honda Civic (I have only recently said good-bye to mine).

Most teachers are not slouches either. We don't leech the system or receive more than our due, and our three favorite parts of teaching are not June, July, and August. What's lost in the massive chasm between these two stereotypes is the truth. While both saints and slouches undoubtedly work among the millions of American educators, I suspect there exists a silent majority who will never make louche headlines or earn Teacher of the Year (though the latter is certainly something to which many of us aspire).

Against this backdrop I would like to share my perspective on what life is really like for teachers. This is not a salacious tell-all about intra-faculty hookups, embezzled student leadership funds, or smoking behind campus, nor is it a paean to the selfless educator enduring against all odds.

Sure there will be joys, like when Bing belatedly learns of his student's gratitude for altering the course of her life. But there will also be tragedies, like James and Tony attending the funeral of their fallen player, and Dave working unsuccessfully to help free the father of his beloved student from state prison. There will no doubt be embarrassments too, like when Phil accidentally outlines male genitalia during an improvised lesson on gerrymandering and Justin flatulates in front of his students after lunch.

I want to crawl into the cracks and crevices and uncover the sticky bits, the hidden morsels so often overlooked or deemed unworthy of genuine examination—to plumb the depths of our profession, good, bad, and otherwise, because anything less would be misleading.

I also hope these essays will ring true for my colleagues. The rhythms of a semester, the challenges with grading, the exhilaration from a well-executed lesson, the private truths revealed behind the closed doors of the lunchroom, whispered in the halls, and chanted at year-end teacher parties. We spend the majority of our working lives isolated from adults yet surrounded by teenagers, which can lead to strange behaviors and a unique worldview.

The precious hours we do share with colleagues blowing off steam and seeking advice become hugely important, almost sacred. And though we encourage kids to act like adults, more often than not the opposite is true when teachers get together (gather teachers for a Monday afternoon staff meeting and watch what happens).

Most of all I want to illustrate the simple yet overlooked notion that teachers are people. People with lives both inside and outside the classroom. In doing so, I hope to improve our education system by *humanizing* the teaching profession. I believe strongly in education's power to liberate individuals and advance society, and I think there is great benefit in understanding the often-misunderstood career that I love so much. So come see what it's actually like to be a teacher! I think it may surprise you.

Acknowledgments

Thanks to my editor Tom Koerner for his insight and vision, without which this book surely would not have come to be, and to the entire team at Rowman & Littlefield for their eminent expertise and professionalism. Thanks as well to my uncle Stephan Bodian for his thoughtful attention during the early stages of this manuscript; and to my wife Michelle, brother Alex, mom Lini, and dad Jack for their constant support and advice.

To the faculty of Tamalpais High School, especially those with whom I have become close colleagues and friends, I would like to express my deepest gratitude and affection. Apart from offering insight into this book's form and substance, they have served as the inspiration for many of the anecdotes and narratives that fill these pages, helping me understand what it means to teach, and how, and continually renewing my faith in the power and the promise of public education. To my old friend and able photographer Nick Brubaker, thanks for a wonderful cover image; and to Detective Kyle Maxwell of the Mill Valley Police Department, thanks for enabling our entertaining photo shoot.

Finally, thanks to my students past and present who have brought such joy and meaning to my life in the classroom. Teenagers are a never-ending fount of wonderment, and it is a blessing to spend time among them teaching and learning.

Introduction

I spent some time thinking about the ideal structure for this book. Neither memoir nor textbook seemed quite right, and eventually I settled on a collection of essays grouped by theme. You might also call these essays chapters, as each builds toward and is related to a controlling idea, the case for which I have made in the preceding preface.

The essays themselves are composed of stories woven with commentary. Each features an anecdote along with observations or insights—both to show and to tell, as an English teacher might say—and concludes with bulleted key points.

My aim is to animate ideas rather than dispassionately dissect them; to enliven teachers' daily experiences and considerations, no matter how big or small, serious or irreverent, personal or professional, in a way that's engaging but also informative. And I think narrative essays, linked in purpose and assembled by theme, is the most effective vehicle for doing so.

The first section, "The Art and Craft Part I," addresses issues traditionally related to instruction; the second, "The Lunchroom," discusses the significance of colleagues to one's practice; the third, "The Art and Craft Part II," returns to instruction but tackles those aspects lesser known and frequently ignored; the fourth, "In Loco Parentis," examines the impact of parents; the fifth, "Student, Scholar, Teenager, Kid," considers students, though students will occupy many if not most of these pages; and the sixth section, "More than a Classroom Teacher," highlights elements of teaching taking place outside the classroom but within the scope of the job.

And now let's get on with the show.

Section I

THE ART AND CRAFT PART I

Chapter 1

Late for Class

Derek is late for class on the first day of school, running through a small courtyard of orange trees. The sun has recently risen over the surrounding hills, splashing rosy light against four doors and a trickling fountain. Dashing left to right, like Pac Man, he approaches three of the entrances in succession but they are closed.

Sixty seconds shy of the opening school bell, he pulls on the fourth door, big and blue, but it's locked as well. Having run from the lower parking lot up three sets of stairs he squeegees his forehead with an index finger and gazes upon a haunting scene. Dozens of teenagers are staring at him through diaphanous glass.

The bell rings as students pivot and disperse. Pressing his face against the window, Derek peers toward backpacks fleeing down a long hallway. Suddenly, with a soft click, a female arm appears. It recedes into collapsing blue but Derek peels back the wooden flap, crosses the threshold, and steps through.

The classroom door opens and Derek encounters an empty whiteboard, puzzling over the disappearance of his agenda and lesson plan. A buzz of voices cuts the silence, signaling the students' return. Some are sitting, others standing, all highly energized, swirling like negatively charged electrons around the nucleus of an unstable atom.

This nightmare, of course, is not real, but a creation of Derek's latent imagination. Most people have it from time to time, the anxiety-induced work dream. The Buddhist monk dreams of arriving to meditations without his robes; the musician dreams of forgetting his mouthpiece and saxophone strap before a gig; the college basketball coach dreams he can't decide what play to draw up during a crucial time-out.

Teachers are no exception. Their dreams often involve riffs on a common theme. Beginning in mid-August and visiting without warning throughout the school year, they arise from a fear of losing control, and control is a prerequisite for any learning and inspiration that is manufactured between bells. Students must feel safe physically, mentally, and emotionally, which is only possible if the teacher is firmly in charge. Teachers may be good at crafting this perception—that's all it really is, after all—but behind the façade lurks an anxious subconscious that emerges during tense nights.

The teacher dream also stems from a natural desire to appear invincible. You can't show weakness, you might believe, can't make a mistake or be unsure of any answer to the countless questions asked every day, week, year, or your authority will diminish and you will lose control. When suppressed long enough, these insecurities surface involuntarily in your sleep.

The classroom noise of Derek's nightmare is dizzying. Students fidget, squirm, and shuffle. A wave of helplessness washes over him, shackling his limbs with paralysis. He's overcome by chattering mouths and flitting eyeballs as he submerges beneath a teenage torrent. Chest heaving, he swallows over short breaths and plunges to new depths of apprehension.

Then an idea strikes: the icebreaker. Derek reaches for balloons, Post-its, and pushpins and soon students are inscribing two truths and a lie on small yellow squares, inserting them into colorfully inflated rubber. But the balloons begin to explode and rainbowed shrapnel litters the room. Kids are standing in the aisles, stepping on pins, facing the wall, texting, texting, texting.

Several students on the periphery attempt to leave. Derek begins to shout and in an instant the noise abates and students are seated each to a desk, a miraculous stillness. Finally, he thinks, their undivided attention.

Before he can speak a faint chuckle echoes in the quiet. It spreads, infecting the entire room. Soon students are howling with laughter. They point on a lowered trajectory in Derek's direction.

He realizes the truth before even looking down and his cheeks flush with blood. Loafers, black socks, shins, knees, thighs, boxer-briefs . . . dress shirt. Exposed, he tugs in vain at the bottom of his dangling button-up.

The laughter is at fever pitch. Adolescent lips quiver with glee at Derek's two bare legs anchored to the classroom floor. He starts to scream but, jaw clenched and teeth gnashing, his mouth is sealed. The walls become unstable and the room begins to pinwheel.

Then he wakes up.

Pantless or not, teachers know losing control in class can be a haunting experience, one that penetrates the very core of their subconscious. When you've lost control, even slightly, it's a naked feeling. You'll do anything to hold those kids' attention. No wonder teaching often feels like a performance—a one-person comedic stand-up routine, a fire-juggling, knife-swallowing, unicycle-riding, high-wire-balancing circus act. Anything to get thirty teenagers to focus. Because if you don't, well, sweet dreams.

KEY IDEAS

- Teaching is a performance; and losing control of students during that performance makes teachers feel vulnerable.
- As a result, teachers often have anxiety-induced dreams about work.

Chapter 2

The Crying Closet

There was once a math teacher from India who won a Fulbright, exchanging positions for one semester with her American counterpart. A kind lady with a warm presence and gentle grace, she recounted genial stories about students in India standing upon their teachers' entrance, often following with applause. Education was not a birthright as in America, she said, the stakes were high, and most kids were grateful for the opportunity to learn.

Call the exchange teacher "Padma." Padma knew her stuff but she was having difficulty controlling a number of students in several sections, particularly intermediate algebra. Padma was coached by her colleagues on differences in the American system and given a few pointers. She had some successes and victories and her experience was generally positive but kids quickly figured out they could ignore her instructions and demands if they wished.

One day toward the end of the semester, in the midst of a slump, Padma was having a particularly difficult time controlling her class. Finally reaching her limit, she walked from the whiteboard between the desks to a closet at the back of the room and shut herself inside.

Soon her students could hear her crying softly. They had proved too much for her, and she was emptied of patience and discipline. She had expected this to be an educational exchange, a journey across the world to witness the beauty of cultural difference through the universal language of mathematics. But the oak-muffled sobs suggested an entirely different experience altogether. If only those kids would listen!

Considering Padma in her closet, you probably cannot help feeling sympathy and indignation. You might picture her alone in the dark, thousands of miles from home, separated from a bitter reality by shelves, hangers, and a thin wooden door. Shouldn't her students have listened, for once just paid attention? Didn't they understand their position as cultural ambassadors?

Undoubtedly they did not. Though teenagers are often more obstreperous and less rational than adults, like all people they respond to their environment, which in education is largely teacher-generated. The issue of fault in this case misses the point. By developing strong classroom-management skills, teachers can avoid the Crying Closet and in the process maintain peak engagement, which is a cornerstone of learning.

So how do you control a room of adolescents armed solely with your voice and a few incentives? There are several principles and techniques that form the basis of a well-managed class—almost like venerable basketball coach John Wooden's Pyramid of Success. Call it the Engagement Triangle (or not).

Now imagine a most difficult student named Kenny. Kenny deals drugs, wears flashy shades, often carries a skateboard, and some days even shoulders a boombox. Often disruptive, he's also slippery and intelligent, the kind of adolescent who requires a teacher's gaze at all times and thus his teacher Issa's entire arsenal of classroom-management weapons.

Today Issa is teaching a social studies lesson on drug awareness as part of a larger health and wellness unit. She's about to start class when Kenny swaggers in late with sunglasses in his hand and a skateboard tucked like a football under his arm.

She tries to remember the first principle of classroom management: Be Yourself. This is both the easiest and hardest to master. If you seem inauthentic and don't know who you are, students will not follow. But if they like you they will work for you, and when students are on your side, life in the classroom is much easier.

"Good morning, everyone. Happy Tuesday. Highs today in the 70s. Fog should burn off by the afternoon."

Still standing, Kenny pretends he can't find his seat.

Time for the second principle: Confidence; or Cool, Calm, and Collected. Like bees and dogs, kids sense weakness, they smell fear. Being poised puts others at ease so it's important to project an aura of self-confidence even where none exists. Rather than creeped-out or on edge, if students feel comfortable around you they are more likely to respond positively, and learn. It's not just Kenny in the room, remember, but twenty-nine other students equally deserving of Issa's attention. If one kid rattles her they all suffer.

"Kenny, have a seat please. Thank you."
"Where?"
"You know where."

Still standing.
"Kenny."

He glares at Issa with an expressionless face and lively eyes. Her heart beats faster and she stares right back. This is not their first tango, her and Kenny, so she contemplates deploying either nuclear weapon in her arsenal: the Referral or Detention. While sending Kenny to the assistant principal's office or requiring additional work after school might temporarily correct his behavior, the craters of animosity and mushroom clouds of resentment will almost ensure mutual relationship destruction. (Plus sending Kenny from class might be exactly what he desires, namely, freedom from the yoke of academic exertion.)

Referrals are also particularly dangerous for young teachers seeking permanence because it's important admin believes they can solve their own problems—or better yet that none exist. So remember rule number two, and stay cool.

Time for Issa's big girl voice.

"Ke—"
"Oh yeah, right here. Sorry."

He grins and finds his seat in front of her, as if sensing the exact limits of her patience, and places his skateboard wheels down beneath the desk. (She can deal with that later if necessary.) Kenny clearly doesn't like his Selective Seating Chart but, given his behavior during the first month of school, Issa has placed him at the front of class where she can teach hovering directly above his desk.

Believe it or not, Desk Arrangement has a big effect on behavior and learning. Possibilities include rows, groups, a horseshoe, even a cluster. Issa opts for the shotgun formation featuring two mirroring rows on either side of class because having students face each other seems to foster a sense of togetherness and, most important, she can physically reach each student. Plus by pacing up and down the barrel, so to speak, there is no back of class. Try hiding now, dear Kenny.

Issa then reviews the agenda and gives instructions for a "jigsaw" activity involving the creation of drug-specific presentations, and most students assemble into groups. Except, of course, for Kenny, who she sticks with three high-functioning young women. Though not pleased, they accept the news gracefully. Kenny needs workers who'll keep him on task and Issa is hoping this Selective Grouping will help the next portion of class run smoothly.

At her desk, Issa takes roll and a quick break, only to notice Kenny now wearing his sunglasses. Calling his name will disrupt the collective focus so she needs a more nuanced response. Issa decides to walk the room and see how various groups are progressing, waiting for Kenny to look in her direction.

When Kenny finally glances over she swipes at her eyes, removing an imaginary pair of shades. It's a subtle redirection, one Issa is hoping will work the first time. But Kenny turns toward his group and feigns ignorance. *At least he's pretending to participate*, she thinks, which is an improvement over distracting others.

Again Issa pantomimes taking off her sunglasses while Kenny responds with the same nonplussed countenance.

"Kenny, nice work but you need to remove those glasses."
"Why? I can still see."
"Take them off or hand them over. Your call."

It's a necessary ultimatum with some risk. If he refuses the situation could escalate to the realm of Detention or Referral.

Fortunately Kenny stands down, placing the sunglasses on his desk.

When groups have completed their presentations, including slides for a visual aid, Issa distributes a note-taking grid to hold students accountable for the upcoming information. This is a cheap trick to maintain focus but, especially for a young teacher, not unwise. It's also an example of the final principle: Content Drives Classroom Management.

If students know they will be held accountable for learning, that the class is serious and academic, they will pay attention. What's more when the subject is relevant, even exciting, it's difficult for students to drift and disengage. Genuine learning at its best is fun.

Content and the associated grades, however, may also become a threat. This isn't ideal but in certain situations, particularly for inexperienced teachers, it can be necessary. Though less desirable than making curriculum engaging, content-as-threat is effective for using the coursework to keep students focused and under control. So, class, you're taking notes during the jigsaw and that's that.

As various groups discuss heroin, cocaine, and now methamphetamine, most students follow intently while several appear distracted—in large part because Kenny is making noises from his desk—but Issa doesn't want to disrupt the overall flow. So instead she fires a red-hot gaze in his direction: the Look of Death. Her brow is furrowed, her lips pursed, eyes dark. Eventually Kenny peeks at Issa and is caught in her visual tractor beam boring deep into his soul. They lock eyes for an uncomfortable moment before Issa releases with a stern headshake. Her face says what her lips cannot. Don't mess around, man.

The presentations continue as do Kenny's interruptions. It becomes clear he has a cursory, street-level understanding of many drugs but is missing important nuance and detail. Though many students are writing consistently,

Issa reminds the class to make thorough notes because some have lost focus and need the extra prompting. Kenny understands the directions but simply refuses. *We'll see about that,* she thinks. *We'll see who wins this battle. Just wait for my ace in the hole.*

When all groups have finished Issa pulls the room together for the last few minutes, though Kenny has already begun to pack up and chat with his neighbor. While debriefing the lesson Issa walks from the back of class to the front. Often Teacher-Positioning near a talkative student is enough to quiet him.

But Kenny is still chatting, causing others to look in his direction. While addressing the entire group, Issa Taps a Finger on his desk. He looks up, only to continue talking.

She pauses mid-sentence. For some this concluding discussion has become white nose beside the approaching bell but now the silence is booming.

Still waiting.

Sixty eyeballs are trained on the front of the room. Or rather fifty-eight. Issa's use of the Pregnant Pause has worked for almost everyone.

She considers a Selective Query—asking Kenny the final question to get his attention—but doesn't want to push too hard. They've both had enough for the day.

As students begin to leave, Issa once more approaches Kenny.

"Hey wait up a sec. We need to have a few words."

This move is the Hold, her ace in the hole, and Kenny is now cringing. Clutching his skateboard and sunglasses, he can't believe he might miss his buddies' excursion off campus for lunch. Even if he isn't listening and her encouragement doesn't sink in, at least in the future Kenny will weigh his disobedience against the potential reduction of his break.

"I know you have the ability but we need to see a better effort," Issa says. "I don't want to hold you after anymore, but we have to see a change. Okay?"

He nods.

"*Okay?*"

"Okay."

"All right, have a good lunch. See you Thursday."

Fortunately this day Kenny doesn't drive Issa to the Crying Closet. She's able to channel the three principles of the Engagement Triangle: Be Yourself, Have Confidence, and Content Drives Classroom Management. Along with Desk Arrangement Issa also uses strategies like a Selective Seating Chart and Selective Grouping, Teacher Positioning, the Look of Death, the Finger Tap, the Pregnant Pause, and the Hold. Thankfully the Referral and Detention aren't necessary.

But consider Kenny is one student in a pretty good class. Envision several Kennys, picture he comprises a third to a half of your class, and you can imagine how Padma must have felt.

In the end, it may remain a mystery why she entered her wooden cabinet, induced to tears by an unruly section of intermediate algebra. Though from time to time all teachers want to hide in the closet, good classroom management offers more than shelter from despair. It creates the space for inquiry and reflection.

Classroom management is important because it's necessary for student learning, which is the ultimate goal of any teacher. Except—and here's the wrinkle—just because students are quiet doesn't necessarily mean they're paying attention. Compelling students to listen is just the beginning. Now you must get them to learn.

KEY IDEAS

- Classroom management is a requisite precursor to good instruction.
- Classroom management is a learned skill, the constituent elements of which include three principles (Be Yourself, Have Confidence, Content Drives Classroom Management) and a number of specific techniques (Desk Arrangement, Selective Seating Chart, Selective Grouping, Teacher Positioning, Referral, Detention, the Look of Death, the Finger Tap, the Pregnant Pause, the Hold).

Chapter 3

Design and Conquer

Today is a good day in World History. Stephanie is putting Napoleon Bonaparte on trial. The classroom is divided into three circles, each with two prosecution and defense attorneys and three to five jurors. Stephanie asks lawyers from the French Republic to rise and a silent tension fills the air. Students have spent about half an hour preparing for this moment.

"Are you ready for opening statements?"

The young litigants nod.

"You may proceed."

She raps her wooden gavel against its sound block and the students begin outlining evidence they will present against the little man from Corsica, proving beyond any reasonable doubt his betrayal of the revolution. *Ladies and gentlemen of the jury, the evidence will show . . .*

"Thirty seconds," Stephanie calls out after three minutes or so.

"Aaaaaand stop!"

Perorations concluded, attorneys high-five their partners and sit down. Next is the defense's opening statement. Then a presentation of the evidence. The room is full of excited voices disputing Napoleon's disastrous invasion of Russia and ultimate defeat at Waterloo, his creation of a meritocracy and the Napoleonic Code. They call as imaginary witnesses Voltaire, Robespierre, Jean Paul Marat.

Stephanie's plan for today's class is constructed on the foundation of a similar lesson from her mentor teacher. A culture of collaboration permeates the faculty and her mentor has given Stephanie most of his curriculum—a veritable document dump, a massive leak.

Buried among electronic folders of units, activities, and assessments lies the Holy Grail: a World History calendar outlining a concise lesson plan for each day of the semester. During her first years of teaching it proves an invaluable road map; sometimes she follows it religiously, other times borrowing and stealing like an uncertain agnostic.

When Stephanie was a younger teacher she had assumed a quiet room meant focused students. Now not necessarily so. It's easy for the mind of a motionless body to float up and away, out the window and into another universe. Attention and engagement are valuable, fleeting commodities and neither laughter nor stillness are complete indicators of their existence. Both the entertainer and the tyrant must make sure their students are paying attention. Depending on the purpose, a classroom might range from frenetic to humming to silent all in a single period.

This particular lesson has endured several iterations and Stephanie is once again trying something different. Students arrived to class having read several pages about Napoleon's dramatic rise to power and equally spectacular fall (true, writing lacking a strong narrative or compelling argument can be dry but textbooks are also clear, concise, at grade level, and fairly easy to comprehend). At 8:02 most students are present and she's about to begin class. She welcomes everyone and goes over the plan for the day as well as tomorrow's homework, all of which is listed on the agenda down the left-hand side of the whiteboard.

Students are situated and settled and it's time to dive in. Though straightforward from a learner's perspective, this moment is made possible by hours of previous planning. Stephanie has taught World History three times before, so this is her fourth opportunity to teach about Napoleon.

First thing to do is check which kids have completed the homework. The primary purpose of reading, in class or at home, is to *acquire* information. Until neural transmitters are readily available humans must still use their eyes and ears as input devices, so whether via lecture, video, or text, material must somehow enter one's mind.

Students know there are at least two options for demonstrating they have read. They can take notes and show them to Stephanie, or answer a brief quiz she's projected on a screen at the front of the room. She tells herself this should last about five minutes but in reality it takes closer to ten, so she's now about fifteen minutes into a ninety-minute-block period.

This is just the beginning, of course; now she needs to flesh out students' initial understandings, to deepen and push their thinking. As you're likely to appreciate from experience, one understands more fully what they read after talking about it. The information tends to stick longer in one's head. In class, this usually takes the shape of small-group discussions followed by a larger share-out with the entire class so all students can participate while also being guided by the teacher.

Today is slightly different, however, because Napoleon has been charged with crimes against the state. Capital crimes for which, if found guilty, he may face death by the National Razor, the eponymous guillotine invented by Dr. Joseph Guillotine as, of all things, a more egalitarian method of killing compared to previous techniques like drawing and quartering or burning at the stake. Beheadings, students are often interested to know, were once reserved only for the nobility (how easy it is to digress).

In order to draw students in, Stephanie shows the introduction of a PBS documentary. Against panning stills of the cathedral Notre Dame, a choir sings, cymbals crash, and David McCullough narrates Napoleon's coronation. For public television it's stirring stuff. The class seems genuinely interested.

Seizing the moment, she tells students there is great debate among historians about Napoleon's effect on his country's revolution—the first in the history of the world, she emphasizes, to replace a king with a democratically elected government. Sometimes he is cast as saving his country and its new principles from certain internal and external demise, other times as betraying the ideals of *liberté, égalité,* and *fraternité* by merely replacing King Louis XVI with Emperor Napoleon I.

Clearly, much is at stake. Stephanie tries to make the controversy as sensational and dramatic as possible, inserting references to *Lord of the Rings* and Bravo reality television, employing the very best public-speaking techniques at her disposal. She's fired up about this topic and wants students fired up too! Reviewing the procedure outlined on the whiteboard, Stephanie assigns groups and takes a quick straw poll to gauge kids' initial judgments, of which about two-thirds would already find Napoleon guilty. Like the citizens of France, these teenagers want blood.

Students select roles and spend about thirty minutes prepping for trial, which includes writing briefs for the lawyers and case summaries for the jurors. Busy at work, most students don't recognize this as a key step in building knowledge—they're simply having fun preparing to compete against their peers. Once finished they're set to apply what they have learned, in this case through a fictitious trial somewhat akin to *Bill and Ted's Excellent Adventure.*

After students give opening statements and call imaginary witnesses the trial ends where it began, with closing arguments.

"Counsels, are you ready to proceed?"

"Yes, your honor."

Ladies and gentlemen, the evidence has shown beyond all reasonable doubt . . .

The three juries then march out of the room to deliberate.

Returning from the hall, they announce their verdicts over a collection of boos and cheers. After the outbursts subside Stephanie debriefs with the entire room and takes another poll. A sizable minority has switched sides and nearly everyone is ardent in their beliefs; several disputes flare up mid-vote and it's clear many students want to continue debating. Unfortunately, class is about to end.

At this point students have read at home, taken notes or a short quiz, written briefs and case summaries, argued in small groups, and discussed overarching themes together as a class. They read, wrote, spoke. The lesson's central goal was for kids to analyze Napoleon's influence on the French Revolution, which has hopefully been accomplished through several different teaching strategies.

There are many exceptions and alternatives, of course, but as a general rule, having students acquire some basic information through reading, make meaning of that information through discussion, and then apply that meaning in a realistic context are the fundamentals of a strong lesson.[1]

A teacher's goals and the strategies to achieve them should be developed prior to instruction, of course. The latter may often change, sometimes minute-to-minute and class-to-class. What works one day with one group might not work the next day with another. Second period is struggling with the trial? Time to audible, switch formations, draw up a Socratic seminar instead. *How* to realize your objectives, the means rather than the end, often fluctuates frequently, which makes it important to be mindful about the specific methods you will decide to use.

Yet constant reflection is both a blessing and a curse. Should you assign reading for homework or as an activity in class? Is note taking even necessary? How about annotating photocopies or simply reading instead? How will students prove they've completed it? Which will produce the least cheating? Should kids pick their own small groups or should you select for them? Do they have to write legal briefs on the same subject or is that too repetitive? Are the expectations of lawyers and jurors sufficiently equal? Do they need to be?

Furthermore, should jurors be required to speak as much as the attorneys? Is a trial really the best vehicle to drive student understanding about Napoleon's reign? In addition to the subject matter, have students improved any of their academic skills? How might one stretch the higher-end kids while making sure those in need of extra support actually receive it? What should be done before and during the trial while kids are working in groups? How does this lesson square with the overall sequence of the unit, the semester, and the year?

Limitless are the questions a teacher might ask about curriculum planning. But then again maybe the question *is* the answer. Regular reflection is essential, especially with a colleague or peer, otherwise one's practice will never improve. Planning lessons is teachers' bread and butter, it's what they do, and a rising tide of good instruction lifts everyone's boat. Indeed, sound preparation can be the lifeline of a struggling educator, young or old.

While a teacher's disposition, personal relationships with students, and academic expertise matter a great deal, it is his or her skill at creating and delivering lessons that may be most impactful of all on student learning.

So as Napoleon might say were he a principal rousing his staff: design well, my teachers, and you shall conquer.

Also, beware the Russian winter.

KEY IDEAS

- Lesson planning and delivery are among the most important teacher-controlled factors affecting student learning.
- A good lesson template involves students obtaining information, constructing, and then applying knowledge.
- Ongoing reflection, especially about lesson design and implementation, is essential to one's teaching practice.

NOTE

1. Two alternatives involve learning through larger projects, either wall-to-wall or at the end of a unit of study. The first means introducing the project—like creating a news show connecting the lessons of the French Revolution to some current uprising across the globe—and learning all content throughout the process. Hence the name "project-based learning." The second option would be assigning Revolutions News Hour as an assessment at the end of the unit for students to show what they have learned. This could be referred to as problem-based learning, as in, "Hey—we have a problem: the Middle East is on fire and we need to consult history to determine how best to put it out."

Chapter 4

Teaching Is Coaching

It's the first full week of practice after making cuts, and Coach is teaching his players a very simple concept: how to get open on the wing. A fundamental skill drilled into young athletes since youth leagues, it's something his players already should have known, but Coach doesn't take it for granted. He understands all players are beginning the season with varying abilities, that what might be new for some is second nature to others, and he wants to make sure everyone hears it from him at least once.

Alex is a rookie teacher and Coach's assistant, listening from beyond the three-point arc. In the span of a few short hours, Alex will come to realize he can learn as much about teaching by helping Coach as he can in an entire credentialing program.

Coach stands at the free-throw line, clutching his whistle. A row of players waits at the wing, another below the basket.

"Okay, let's get going," he says. "We'll begin with the V cut. Use this if you're quicker than your defender. Start at the three-point line, walk him down, make contact and pop out."

After clearly explaining the move—what teachers might call direct instruction—Coach then takes a few steps back and demonstrates the cut, modeling for his team the proper technique. He walks deliberately to the low block then flashes quickly to the wing, showing off his aging but still-explosive first step.

"Got it, guys? Pretty simple. Jimmy and Brendan, step out. Jimmy, get open. Brendan, you're on D."

He flips Alex a basketball at the top of the key. Alex waits for Jimmy to execute a proper V cut then throws him a pass on the wing.

"Good," Coach says. "Jimmy, remember: give Coach a target and show your outside hand."

At this point players should understand the cut; but there's a big difference between *knowing* how to do something and actually being *able* to do it. So after both examples, one solo from Coach and the other run more quickly with two players, the team drills several times. Coach then repeats the steps for the L cut and seal, the three traditional methods of creating space on the wing. In this way players are able to apply their newfound knowledge, to practice what they've just learned in a controlled environment.

The next drill, though, is live.

"Game speed now. Remember to choose the right move: the V if you're quicker than your defender, the L if it's even and the seal if you're slower. Defenders, don't let him get it." From each line, one player steps out to begin.

"Good, Spencer. Take him all the way down, nice work. Next."

Another pair.

"Good."

Another.

"Good!"

And then something inside Alex clicks, the threads of an idea weaving together. He realizes coaching basketball is very much like teaching. That in fact teaching *is* coaching. Before each practice, Coach withdraws from his binder a practice plan much like the lesson plans Alex stays up late each night to complete. In unnervingly exact penmanship Coach lists activities along with their estimated times, including his reminders and practice goals. A goal for each lesson, Alex thinks, is probably something he should be doing in class.

Alex also realizes Coach's practices feature many of the abstract elements of good instruction he's been learning about in his credentialing program, which essentially boil down to this: explain something, model it, practice it, then apply it in a real-world context.

Coach is teaching how to get open on the wing while Alex is busy fumbling through a sloppy African storytelling project. But it's starting to make a little more sense. Alex wants his freshmen to be able to perform an engaging folktale, to become aspiring griots and bards. What can he do tomorrow in class to get back on track?

Alex decides to teach public speaking like getting open on the wing. He'll explain the elements of effective voice and body language—like volume, pacing and inflection, gestures, posture and eye contact—then model a performance for students, maybe with a fable like "Why the Cheetah's Cheeks Are Stained." Next, students will practice with a partner, providing constructive criticism to one another after each story as Alex circles the room, listening in. Kind of like the V, L, and seal cuts the team has been practicing.

If this speaking activity is akin to Coach's wing entry drill, Alex wonders if the folktale performance, the assessment, will be the game. The basketball team regularly plays in front of large crowds, so maybe Alex can bring to class an audience of parents, community members, professional raconteur judges, even stage a night of student storytelling at a local café or community playhouse—a live, authentic audience similar to Friday night hoops. Surely there'll be more buy-in from students.

Then a mistake on the court. Coach blows his whistle to deliver some pointed feedback.

"Gino, you're a post player and he's a point guard. Quit running back and forth—you're never gonna get open. Try it again."

Gino runs halfway to the low block, throws a halting shoulder fake and jumps back out, defender on his heels. By the time Alex's pass reaches its target, the smaller guard, in Gino's face like a defensive back, picks the ball and makes for the opposite hoop.

A hush falls over the team, awaiting Coach's apoplectic response. He's going to rip into this kid for sure. But instead he plays it slow, dramatic. Coach tucks his whistle inside his polo shirt and walks toward the wing, stopping in front of the nervous eleventh grader. The tension is thick, the team rapt with fear.

"Gino," Coach begins calmly, his voice low and even. "Who is quicker?"

"Riley."

"That is correct."

"And when the defender is quicker what do you do?"

"The seal move."

"That is also correct. Now let me see you do a seal. Riley, step off."

Gino jogs to the low block, crosses his left foot over his right, spins his back to the basket, sticks out his butt and runs back to the wing. "Very good. See, Gino, I know you know how to do it. Now please repeat that when Riley is guarding you."

"Why is it quiet in here?" Coach glares at both lines, who immediately start clapping.

After Gino correctly executes the move Coach once again blows his whistle.

"Gino, nice work. I want you all to remember: we do things right on this court. If you don't I'm going to let you know. But that's only because I believe we can be great this year, that each one of you has what it takes."

Sly, waiting for the right moment, Coach is using the occasion to remind his team he's demanding yet caring, that he'll hold them to high standards but give everyone ample opportunity to achieve. Seems like something to remember for the classroom, Alex thinks.

In both professions, establishing strong relationships is important above all else. Hard skills and technical expertise are necessary but what's paramount is building bonds with players and students by showing you care about them as people. If you think of your favorite teacher or coach, I'm sure he or she was a talented practitioner but I bet what you remember most, and care about most today, was his or her relationship with you.

Though teachers may have a harder time building strong bonds and serving as role models, these ideals are certainly something to which one can aspire. An inherent advantage of the team over the class is the former's fervent commitment to the shared goal of a championship (as well as its voluntary association).

Teachers often want their classes to be like teams, but this probably won't happen in any meaningful way since any attempt to institute a Championship of Learning would surely fall flat. Instead, teachers can take the best elements of a team and translate them to their class, as well as the best elements of coaching and apply them to their craft.

After Coach's "You've all got what it takes" speech, Gino is quietly enthused. He settles in and practice finds its groove. While the rest of the afternoon is devoted to various fundamental techniques like passing and defensive slides, ultimately culminating in a brief scrimmage, Alex can't help but view it all through a new lens. A similar pattern seems to follow the introduction of each new concept: explain, model, practice and critique, practice and critique some more, then apply.

By the end of practice Alex sees Coach for the educator he is, blending the technical skills of instruction with the ability to motivate, demand, and inspire. Even if the team falls short of a championship, Alex thinks, and his performance in the classroom is far from all-star, through coaching he's learning something about how to teach. From the basketball court he's gleaning lessons for his classroom.

Yet there's still one thing Alex would like to steal from Coach. He can't quite figure it out, and he's not exactly sure how to pull it off, but in class Alex really wants to begin blowing a whistle.

KEY IDEAS

- Teachers can learn a lot from coaches.
- Teaching is like coaching in many ways, including developing a plan of instruction (explain, model, practice, apply), creating real-world assessments, being at once caring and demanding, and inspiring adolescents to greatness through role modeling and building strong relationships.

Chapter 5

Behind the Veil

John Rawls is widely regarded as the preeminent political philosopher of the twentieth century. Harvard professor and author of a number of influential texts, chiefly among them *A Theory of Justice*, Rawls's contribution to modern political theory is unrivaled. But the implications of his work on education reform, in particular educational equity, are quite meaningful too.

With Rawls in mind, consider a teenager named Kevin. Still very much a boy but yearning to be a man, shy, monosyllabic with a heart-melting smile, he's a student Jackson has quickly grown to love. Kevin's dad has been in and out of prison; at this moment he's currently behind bars on gun charges. Since his mom isn't really around either, Kevin is being raised by his grandmother in Section 8 housing.

At some point Kevin's mom has another kid and returns home, living in the same neighborhood near his grandma. Kevin is enamored of his baby brother and his mom lets Kevin stop by regularly. But she uses him as a babysitter, taking advantage of Kevin's fraternal affection, so Grandma forbids Kevin from visiting. On the occasions Kevin cuts school he's actually going to spend time with his little brother.

It's the fall semester and Jackson is teaching a social studies elective about the law. He thinks of Kevin and for some reason Rawls's ideas pop into Jackson's head. Rawls's notions of justice and fairness as the legal groundwork of a society might be interesting to students, Jackson thinks, so he devises an unorthodox method of making Rawls accessible: they'll act out the underpinnings of his theory while having a little fun in the process.

One day in class, after several iterations of lesson planning, kids tape to each other's backs cutouts of hypothetical humans in varying combinations of ethnicity, religion, sexual orientation, socioeconomic status, disability, et cetera—figuratively blindfolding one another, pulling the lever on the bizarrest of imaginary slot machines. Each student shouldn't know the identity of their hypothetical person, Jackson says, nor should they make fun of others for theirs.

Why such a preposterous activity? Because that's Rawls's solution for creating a just society. Rawls asks a fairly straightforward question: if you did not know who you actually were, but had a general notion of the society in which you lived, to what basic rules would you agree in order to ensure a fair shot at a good life? Without knowing, remember, whether you were a member of a privileged or disadvantaged group, whether you would be endowed with very many or very few natural talents and abilities. What basic guidelines, then, would afford you a decent chance no matter your true identity?

Still blindfolded, students eventually arrive at rules quite similar to those of Rawls, which he labels "principles of justice," the moral or philosophical foundation on which all laws in a just society are built. He says there are only two, but since the second has two parts it's really more like three:

First—an equal right to all basic liberties (à la the Bill of Rights).
Second—fair equality of opportunity for all positions (a meritocracy).
Third—any inequalities must benefit the least advantaged (such as social
    safety nets or marginal tax rates).

In many high schools across the country, creating a fair society is not merely a thought experiment. Some schools even educate both the richest and poorest students in America simultaneously, kids with multimillion-dollar parents and those whose moms and dads, if they have relationships with them at all, are in jail. Kind of like Kevin, who happens to be in Jackson's law elective.

Kevin has been struggling mightily, on the verge of failing several times, nearly ineligible to play basketball, seemingly unwilling or unable to learn. He's regularly absent, rarely completes homework and often loses focus in class. Never rude, sweet and frequently withdrawn, Kevin is also reading several grades below level while being raised by a grandmother who can provide only limited support, so his struggles aren't a complete surprise. Yet isn't it his decision to cut class and ignore homework? Isn't he choosing, really, not to learn?

Well what would Rawls say? Rawls would probably deem his first and second principles satisfied since little if any overt discrimination of minorities exists at this school, and because all students have access to the same amount of class time and thus the same quality of instruction. But are these two principles enough? Does Kevin really have a fair chance to succeed? Can he be expected to compete against the upper-middle-class progeny of the neighboring town's parental elite? To this Rawls would answer with an emphatic no.

The reason: rule number three. Both progressive and in some circles controversial, the Difference Principle mandates all inequalities benefit the least advantaged. In the same way more taxpayer money should be spent on the less well-off, students with the greatest need should receive the greatest support. According to Rawls, this is fairness.

How about according to you? If you knew your society but not your identity, if you were situated behind the "veil of ignorance," as Rawls puts it, would these three principles suffice? If you found yourself in a rich family free of historical discrimination, still protected by rules one and two, you'd lose only the financial assistance to the less fortunate. Like an insurance policy, it would protect against the possibility you'd end up among the least advantaged—in which case you're quite grateful for rule number three.

In this light, more is required than simply tolerance and access to the curriculum. Schools are compelled by the principles of justice to go further. One example is summer transition programs between middle and high school; another might be support-centered teaching collaboratives featuring a team of adults assigned to specific students identified as needing extra support, each team including an English and social studies teaching pair, an academic workshop teacher, a tutor, a community liaison, a counselor, and an administrator.

While neither transition programs nor support collaboratives are revolutionary, what both have in common is the desire to provide greater help to those who need it most. These inequalities in funding and assistance would benefit the least advantaged, as Rawls exhorts in *A Theory of Justice*.

Even with some additional support, Kevin struggles. He has a good week then a bad one, a great class then a throwaway. But Kevin never quits—itself a small victory—and in the end he earns a C in Jackson's class. When Kevin learns of his final grade he looks at the floor, bursting with a smile of satisfaction.

Years later Jackson still sees Kevin, a high-school graduate, at basketball games or around town. And Jackson can't help but recall the late New England philosopher whose ideas have the potential to transform educational equity. Not just for Kevin, Jackson thinks, but for so many more.

KEY IDEAS

- John Rawls's ideas as applied to education mean creating fair equality of opportunity for all.
- Rawls's ideas support providing additional resources to students most in need.

Chapter 6

Homework

To Assign or Not to Assign

The question is as timeless as Shakespeare. One that animates human beings young and old alike, its implications weighing upon teachers, parents, and above all, students. A haunting specter, homework can poison families and rip them apart, much like the Hamlets of Denmark. Hence the existential dilemma:

To assign, or not to assign?
That is the question.

Many people would prefer not requiring any homework. Teenagers don't like doing it and teachers don't like grading it. Renowned professors author withering manifestos; venerable publications opine on its crushing effects; students report higher quantities of stress and lower levels of sleep; the pressure to succeed escalates while the likelihood of college acceptance goes down. Yet amid this febrile debate, research about homework's benefits for high schoolers appears mixed. Indeed, something is rotten in the state of education.

The problem is many teachers can't figure out how to avoid it, at least without a sizable loss of learning. Put simply: homework is a necessity though it should be assigned as little as possible. When the final school bell rings students should play, explore, and experience life's many lessons discovered outside the walls of a classroom. On the other hand, private, independent thinking away from others is integral to the learning process, and it also makes class time more productive. In social studies this often means students will read most nights at home.

If students don't read, they will need to acquire new information by watching something or listening to it (how else do ideas penetrate the brain than through the senses?). Though it's possible to manufacture pin-drop silence in class, a home or library is superior since reading is best accomplished in solitude. Home-reading is also "differentiated," or tailored specifically to each kid. Since students read with varying speed and comprehension at different levels of fluency, some will finish quicker than others.

That's fine when one is at home but it creates problems when everyone is together in class. You might be thinking if students are done they can simply begin the next activity—except the next activity is *talking* about what they have read, which is excruciating for those trying to finish. So instead students read outside of school and enter class ready to discuss.

Of course the teenager doth protest too much. When students arrive, teachers need evidence they have done their homework. Annotating or taking notes or a short quiz are all good options. These methods ensure students read and also aid in comprehension à la the "testing effect." Regardless, students should talk about the assignment—and this has to happen in class. There are many ways to facilitate discussions—in small groups, large groups, or as a whole—but the point is something most will intuitively appreciate: it's easier to comprehend what you read after talking about it with other people.

In the next phase of the lesson, social studies teachers design activities asking students to apply what they have read and now discussed. These might include a unit-long project such as making a human rights film, participating in a simulation involving technology and the Industrial Revolution, or learning how to write a Great War research paper like a historian.

Perhaps simplifying learning to "read, talk, do" is overly reductive. But it helps explain why teachers assign homework. In English, for example, it's common to read from a novel at home and interact with it in class. The process is often inverted in math and science—introduce a concept in class and practice it at home. The point is that in order to understand if homework is necessary, it's necessary to understand how people teach and learn.

If you think this is madness, there is method in it.

By now you can infer that if students do not read at home they will have to in class. This means fewer activities, simulations, even movies, all sidelined for the homework now completed at school. Unfortunately, class time really is a zero sum game. Spend eight weeks on a four-week unit and you're now four weeks behind; read for thirty minutes of a ninety-minute class and you'll have one-third less time for everything else. This is why homework, albeit the very least possible, is good for student learning. It also means assignments not meeting this standard should be modified or scrapped altogether.

Alas, frailty, thy name is teacher. You may have moments of doubt, you may regularly question your homework practice, harbor guilt over the stress you cause students and the burden you place on their families. And if a teen-ager should say so in class, these moments will tend to grow.

Imagine a prototypical student, one of your brightest minds, whom we'll call Gracie. She arrives daily to World History with a bright smile and friendly greeting. For Gracie, homework isn't an issue; she loves to read and learn and school is a source of happiness. Early on in your career you assign many more tasks that exceed the "least possible" threshold for take-home work, such as a historical fiction and nonfiction reading project in which kids select from a curated list any book related to the class's themes and, after completing it, write an essay and create an additional artifact.

Gracie choses a novel about the Chinese Cultural Revolution and con-structs a world-class poster. Displayed on a shimmering blue-and-gold avian backdrop are items like a diary, little black shoes, wire-rim glasses, and a brown furry jacket lined with her own meticulous literary analysis. Upon closer examination you notice inscriptions stuffed in and around the other objects like notes in the Western Wall. Gracie must have spent many hours at home on that poster, you think, and you immediately hang it in a prominent location for all to see.

The next year Gracie takes another class you're teaching. You don't assign any homework in part because it's an elective, and those viewed as harder tend to be less popular. Less homework, you think, means more kids register-ing for your class.

Most days begin by talking about current events and how they relate to stu-dents' lives. Since you don't assign homework, students then read and discuss short articles, often followed by brief media clips, transitioning ultimately to some extension activity.

One day halfway through the semester Gracie says, as if steeped in her own thoughts, "I think I'm learning more in this class than I did in World History." She's talking to no one in particular but you overhear it.

At first you're pleased with the value she finds in the course. Then you look above Gracie to her poster with the bird prints, tiny writing, and giant fur jacket. You think about all the extra work Gracie has done in World History compared to this elective. You know she loves history but Gracie is obligated to take it; this time she's here by choice.

Though you can't prove the truth of Gracie's statement, you remain fas-cinated that she may be learning more with less homework. Maybe home-work isn't so important after all, you think. Or maybe student interest and a student-driven curriculum are greater variables in the equation of student learning.

In the end, you have to follow your heart. You don't want students to hate school, you don't want to cause them displeasure, and you don't want to rob them of precious sleep. You want students to enjoy your classes, to learn as much as humanly possible, so you must consider your practice and make decisions based on your training and your beliefs. Above all, to thine own self you must be true.

KEY IDEA

• Homework is often necessary and contributes to student learning, though teachers should assign the smallest amount possible.

Chapter 7

Making the Grade

Marissa waits until most students have left and Michelle is immediately aware of what's coming. They're beginning the penultimate week of the fall semester and Marissa is standing above Michelle's desk with a diffident expression, belying her intense commitment to a high GPA.

"What can I do to improve my grade?" Marissa asks.

Michelle needs to approach this conversation with a light touch because Marissa is deeply invested in her achievement and also because a thoughtless remark might induce an email from Mom and Dad, perhaps even with a copy to Michelle's principal. Marissa is sweet and sometimes goofy and Michelle enjoys her personality, but the pressures to succeed can drive even the nicest teenager to fits of apoplexy. Her question is all too familiar, it's understandable and sometimes even welcomed, except as its frequency increases toward the end of the semester.

Michelle pulls up the gradebook and discovers Marissa has an 88 percent. Ah the B+, Michelle thinks to herself, that most difficult of marks, so close yet so far away. She notices Marissa has had a B for most of September, October, and November, and in the first few weeks of December she's worked to raise it several points. If Michelle says there's nothing Marissa can do Michelle will be viewed as mean, stubborn, and inflexible, so she punts.

"Since you can see all your grades online, what do you think?"

Implying Marissa has already tried to answer this question herself is a bit passive-aggressive, but Michelle smiles and tries to speak warmly.

"I'm not sure exactly but I was hoping you could help, and maybe even tell me why I have a B+?"

Michelle thinks about being as direct as possible, or giving her a compliment sandwich—praise, critique, praise—or trying to deflect the question, or even going into detail about grading schemes, point scales, number-to-letter conversions, and makeups. She wonders if Marissa would be interested in the history.

Prior to computers, teachers kept a physical gradebook. They would ascribe letter grades to specific assignments and, at the end of a semester, look back across the row for a particular student, think holistically about their performance, and determine a score. With the advent of digital processing, however, letter grades could be converted into numbers and thus percentages were born.

But exactly how one converts letters into a number system can be tricky. There are five grades—A, B, C, D, F—so assigning one point to each seems like a good answer, except most electronic grading programs settled on zero through ten or one hundred instead. Hence 90 percent and above is the A range, 80 percent and above the B range, and so on.

Ever consider *why* this is, by the way? Why is an 85 percent and above not an A, for example; why delineate by tens? Categorizing students in quintiles as letter grades or deciles as number grades are both fine, but forcing one into the other can be problematic.

For example, let's assume a student submits a failing essay and another student doesn't turn one in. In the leather-bound gradebook of yore it makes sense the hapless transgressor might receive less credit, a No Mark rather than an F perhaps, but he probably shouldn't be punished doubly. Yet this is precisely what happens in the numeric system because the failing essay earns fifty points and the missing assignment zero.

In effect it counts as a "double F."[1] Or consider four of the five passing letter grades comprise only 40 percent of the scale—sixty through a hundred for D- though A+—while the failing grade gets about 60 percent, or zero through fifty-nine. It seems odd that an F accounts for over half the numeric scale yet only 20 percent of the alphabetic one.

At the beginning of the year Michelle explained her grading system to Marissa's class, so Marissa is likely to understand four points are allotted to missing ten-point assignments, while sometimes the ten-point scale is forgone altogether. While this is perhaps the most technical issue to consider when creating a digital gradebook, there are several others to keep in mind, like categories and weighting.

For instance, if you're going to use a point method, does every point count the same? Do you simply enter assignments throughout the semester and observe what your computer says are students' final percentages at the end? If there are 986 total points and Marissa gets 838 then she has earned an 85 percent and thus a B.

If you're going to use this omnibus method you need to be very careful to distribute points evenly, because if the French Revolution unit is worth 302 points and the Imperialism unit 159, and you value both equally, your grading system will be inaccurate. And in addition to discrete units of content, if all points are not created equal you must decide how to distribute them among tests, projects, homework, participation, et cetera.

Michelle is currently using two equally weighted categories, Process and Performance. The former includes all homework, in-class activities, and "formative" assessments while the latter includes all "summative" or final assessments like tests, quizzes, and projects. The rationale seems straightforward because both categories are equally important and equally reflective of a student's learning.

Take Marissa. She's an assiduous student, she works hard and completes nearly every note-taking assignment thoroughly; however she also possesses below-average literacy skills and struggles to identify main ideas and support them with sufficient detail. She makes thorough notes for homework, speaks both superficially and with insight during class discussions, and struggles mightily on exams. "I'm just a really bad test taker," she says, though Michelle remains unsure which evidence is the truest reflection of Marissa's knowledge.

Perhaps it's a mix of both. If she earns a 93 percent in the Process category and an 83 percent in Product, what grade does she deserve? Averaging the two equals 88 percent—her grade one week prior to the semester's end and the reason she's currently standing in front of Michelle—and thus a B+ on her final transcript and three grade points instead of four.

But maybe categories shouldn't be used in this sense at all. Michelle could simply assign a grade for each unit of study and then average those unit grades for a final mark at the end of the semester. Marissa has worked through three units in World History, for example, and is about to finish her fourth: Rise of Democracy, Revolutions, Industrialization, and Imperialism. Each could be worth one hundred points, or less depending on its relative size and significance.

Or Michelle could dispense with the notion of points altogether and revert to letter grades instead. At the end of each unit, looking at all her assessments including homework, class discussions, activities, tests, and projects, Michelle could give Marissa the grade Michelle believes Marissa deserves based on the evidence Michelle has collected—not what a computer says is correct.

If at the end of the semester Marissa has an A- for the first unit, a B for the second, a B- for the third and an A for the fourth, Michelle will use these scores to determine her final grade; an interesting combination of old-school and new-age methods.

Though Michelle doesn't want to admit as much to Marissa, it's clear that grading is inherently imprecise. After all, it's difficult to enter the mind of another person. Teachers' attempts to do so also don't occur uniformly;

there are myriad ways of measuring learning. Since formal grading systems are prone to error, teachers regularly accommodate, make exceptions, give students the benefit of the doubt. Whatever the particulars, most teachers will agree grading systems should be fair, accurate, and designed to improve student learning.

By now Marissa has been waiting patiently for an answer. What can she do to improve her grade? Michelle thinks about leveraging her aspirations for an A and decides she can have other opportunities to improve because those opportunities will yield greater learning—which is the point. Marking retakes and makeups in addition to the regular paper flow, however, requires time.

Consider this: if an essay takes five minutes to read and score and you teach three sections of twenty-five students, grading one assignment will last *over six hours.* Nearly an entire day's work. And you still have two other classes to contend with. Even though most teachers don't assign weekly essays, grading assignments in general and writing in particular gobbles up an enormous amount of time.

Which is why teachers often "take their papers for a ride." Lost in a desert of student work, one can be lured by the weekend's mirage of additional time. Many are the Fridays you assure yourself this Saturday and Sunday will be different, but barbeques and music lessons and groceries and laundry bleed quickly into Monday morning. The papers have traveled from your classroom to your car and, if you're lucky, your kitchen table—only to chart the same course in reverse and land, ungraded, back in your inbox, awaiting another Friday and their next journey. The frequent flier miles could take you to Europe.

So while empowering Marissa to reach for the A is probably wise, it's going to create some extra work for Michelle, especially this late in the semester. But Marissa is saying she wants to try. Michelle wonders about the other students who aren't as proactive; she's torn between wanting to support Marissa and feeling the need to be unbiased.

Michelle is about to reveal her answer when she's arrested by metaphor. Teachers, it seems, are like defense attorneys and judges rolled into one. It's odd to be a fierce advocate for students while simultaneously rendering judgment on their performance.

Michelle genuinely cares about the success of all her kids and her heart says give everyone A's—but her mind recognizes the importance of awarding each their due. As her advocate, Michelle wants to hand Marissa the A because she likes her and she's proud of her diligence this semester; but as her judge this rationale alone feels incomplete.

Supreme Court Justice Ben Cardozo famously asked, "What is it that I do when I decide a case?" The same question could be put to teachers: What is it they do when they grade? Justice Cardozo explained judging is more than merely "matching colors," or finding applicable precedents and affixing them to the facts at hand. Evaluating students is also not simply a matter of totaling points and assigning the corresponding percentage or letter.

Michelle could explain to Marissa that teachers and judges reach decisions based on the evidence before them. While a judge might consider eyewitness testimony, forensic DNA, or security camera footage, a teacher thinks about test scores, essay grades, project work. Both consider the totality of the circumstances—every shred of information reflects on guilt or innocence, B+ or A-. There is no single rule for judges to follow when they render a verdict; not all precedents clearly and equally align with the facts of a case, and it's often impossible to simply "match colors."

As Justice Cardozo says, this is where the real jurisprudence begins. Likewise there is no generally accepted science on grading. One wants to gather a range of evidence—a collage rather than a snapshot—in order to construct the fullest picture, but how evidence is collected, and what shape it takes, varies widely. Judges and teachers alike want to make decisions that are fair and accurate and structured to improve the well-being of those before them.

Marissa is beginning to stir. She wishes Michelle would stop talking about lawyers and the Supreme Court and just give her an answer already. She's more than likely not questioning why judges' verdicts are more fully accepted after trial than teachers' report cards at the end of a semester.

This is because judges are afforded greater deference in our society—partly since it's tough to become one and also as they're required of a healthy democracy. But our education system would improve if teachers were similarly trusted and respected, and raising the bar so it's more difficult to enter the field is one of several possible solutions.

In the end, Michelle channels both defense attorney and magistrate. Looking at Marissa's grades, she discovers Marissa fared poorly during the Industrialization unit so Marissa decides to make up her in-class essay. She has shown great effort and Michelle wants to provide her every opportunity, reward her hard work. She also tells Marissa she won't just give her the A—she'll have to earn it.

After Michelle sees Marissa's essay she'll take it into consideration when evaluating the corpus of Marissa's work. She'll weigh all evidence of her learning and make a final decision. Justice won't be blind in this case because Michelle is pulling for Marissa, but she knows it will be fair. At least Michelle will do her very professional best to make it so.

Three weeks later Marissa bursts into Michelle's room between first and second period. It's the first day back from Winter Break.

"You gave me an A!" she exclaims, hopping ever so slightly, fingers balled into fists.

"I didn't give you anything," Michelle says with a smile. "You earned it."

KEY IDEAS

- Grading systems should be fair, accurate, and designed to improve student learning.
- There are a number of technical issues to consider when grading, such as point scales, categories, number-to-letter conversions, zeros, and second chances.
- Like attorneys and judges, teachers fervently support students while simultaneously weighting evidence of their learning to determine final grades.

NOTE

1. Credit for this idea goes to Douglas Reeves. A more detailed explanation can be found in his article "The Case Against the Zero," *Phi Delta Kappan* (December 2004).

Chapter 8

Teaching Tupac; or, Outposts of Affluence

Many problems in American education are reflections of society at large. Two of the biggest are poverty and inequality. Countless studies have shown socioeconomic status ranks among the biggest predictors of educational achievement, and the combination of inequality at record highs and social mobility at a near-all-time low is a recipe for disaster. At their best, schools are a place to level the playing field, to nudge all students closer to the starting line in order to have a more equal opportunity to compete—and succeed.

In many ways, Tamalpais High in Mill Valley, California, is a model school. Less than a thirty-minute drive north from San Francisco across the Golden Gate Bridge, its peach-colored buildings dot the slope of Mount Tamalpais—known to locals as the Sleeping Lady because of her elegant supine profile, literally the peak on which mountain biking was invented. Top-ranked and high-performing, even idyllic, Tam nonetheless suffers from a stubborn achievement gap, an issue well known to many other schools in the country.

Tam also represents a number of distinct communities: Mill Valley, Sausalito, Marin City, Stinson, and Bolinas, a diversity that creates both beauty and conflict. The school is a social petri dish that, when cultured, grows into something unique. Plus, it claims a very famous alum.

Before going on to international stardom as both a recording artist and actor, Tupac Shakur used to freestyle rap outside Tam's drama building before class. He also refused to have his picture taken for the yearbook because he knew someday he'd become a celebrity. Occasionally photos of him around campus will emerge on social media.

Tupac's home for a few short years was Marin City, which formed during World War II when many African Americans relocated from the South to find work at the shipyards in now tourist-friendly Sausalito. Unfortunately, many also discovered racism in this liberal enclave and were subtly encouraged—if not formally instructed—to live in a quasi-separate municipality.

Future Supreme Court justice Thurgood Marshall even argued a case involving the shipyard and trade union freedoms for African Americans, *James v. Marinship*, securing an early victory in the civil rights movement. Today the lower socioeconomic status of many Marin City students is manifested in poorer graduation and college attendance rates. This achievement gap is arguably the greatest problem facing Tam since, unlike Tupac, not everyone can be successful without a degree.

Bolinas, like Stinson Beach, is an artist colony, a close-knit community brimming with creativity and imagination, and a disproportionate number of notable poets, where locals famously remove all entrance signs to their furtive Eden. To be in Bolinas is to be elsewhere, special.

Most of Tam's students, however, come from Mill Valley, which on several occasions has been voted among the best places to live nationally—though it has also drawn popular mockery for its liberal upper-middle-class ethos, like the South Park "Smug Alert!" episode, which was based on it. Yes, hybrids choke the streets, but parent clubs also raise generous funds and lavish schools with tremendous support. And perhaps most important, Mill Valley homes, with some of the country's highest property values, provide tax revenue that sustains the district, making it one of the better funded in California.

So how are students from these starkly varied backgrounds supposed to collaborate and compete in the classrooms of Tam? Many Marin City students will begin at a distinct disadvantage, while many from Sausalito and Mill Valley will have every opportunity, and those from Stinson and Bolinas will fall somewhere in between.

Since Marin City comprises less than 10 percent of Tam's population, and Bolinas-Stinson about the same, each class might have one to two black kids and one or two from the beach, plus a smattering of Asians and Latinos. The vast majority will be well off and white. This modest diversity leads to an interesting learning environment but creates major challenges as well.

For instance, how do you determine the rigor of your class? How much reading and writing should you assign, and how hard should you grade? Is homework justifiable when some kids clearly have more parental support than others? If three-quarters of students are anxious to gallop while the rest are learning to walk, how slack are your reins? Do you shoot for some arbitrary middle and differentiate instruction for the bottom and top? And if one student is reading at a fifth-grade level, how can he possibly keep up with his peers?

The point is not to snuff out all disadvantage and privilege but rather to create equal opportunity, a true meritocracy in which all students receives their due. Public schools are the gateway to the American dream. They should exhibit structures to counteract societal inequality while also striving for excellence and embracing competition. When students walk through the schoolhouse doors, they should be challenged and pushed, and supported as needed with extra resources like layered teacher support, extended library hours, and off-campus tutoring, to name only a few.

There are certainly more questions than answers. But it's important for schools like Tam to contemplate how best to serve *all* their communities, maintaining difficult academic standards, producing the leaders of tomorrow, while also providing adequate support for those who need it most today.

If the classroom were a sports team, the student with a fifth-grade reading ability would be cut. Only schools aren't in the business of cutting—they exist to ensure all students have a fair crack at the American dream. Because at the end of the day, the goal is to keep all kids in the game.

KEY IDEAS

- School should be a place where students have equal opportunity to compete and succeed.
- Schools serve and reflect unique communities, which necessarily impacts how their students learn and how their teachers teach.

Section II

THE LUNCHROOM

Chapter 9

Sticker Shock

Imagine a young teacher on his first day of his first full year of teaching. Peter has successfully navigated three classes and it's now time for lunch. Believe it or not, this is a momentous decision. Peter can eat alone, try the downstairs break room—both miserable options—or join the group in the class next door.

He's been warned by several people, including his department chair and assistant principal, that the members of this group were not to be trusted, that they talked trash, spread rumors, and held a certain reputation with much of the faculty and administration. A little shady if respectable, they're certainly not a crowd with whom he wants to be associated. Especially as a first-year teacher vying someday for a permanent position, he's told, eating with them might be risky. Except in Peter's mind they seem pretty cool.

Thus very quickly he's faced with a choice: betray his department chair and an administrator, both of whom hold his professional fate in their hands, or enter the room next door. This isn't an academic question but a decision with real consequences, since he doesn't want to end up like the nearly half of all new teachers who quit within their first five years due to loneliness and isolation—not because of money. (Those who point to the low percentage of terminated teachers overlook this ruthlessly high turnover rate.)

"Come eat with us," says Jane.

Jane helped Peter corral textbooks during the initial teacher workday, and from her first sarcastic remark he hoped they'd be friends.

Peter is rambling from the bathroom back to his class when she extends the invitation. Eating alone seems the safest play but after three hours with teenagers some adult time is desperately needed. Not like he was going to barge in uninvited though.

"Let me grab my sandwich," he says.

43

Upon entering he recognizes a few familiar faces, but for several reasons he's still not at ease. Not only is this his first day teaching, it's also an early attempt at dressing smartly. A sartorial tenderfoot, he's recently visited a discount department store and purchased what he thinks are several stylish yet sensible slacks plus a pair of black loafers.

The conversation begins pleasant enough.

"Can't believe we're back already."

"Seems like summer just started."

"Today was a little rough in the classroom."

"Yeah, kind of a shock."

"But it's great to see everyone again."

"I know. Missed you guys."

Hesitant to interject he quietly eats his lunch, taking in the different faces, the energy, the flow. Sated from potato chips and a homemade ham sandwich he slouches back in his chair with legs extended, loafer soles exposed to the group in that most offensive of Arab insults.

Then he notices Jane sniggering with another teacher named Mark in highly sophomoric fashion across the room. They're clearly talking about someone. When Mark throws a furtive head nod in Peter's direction it becomes clear Peter is the butt of their humor. That's pretty rude, trash-talking the new guy on his first day, he thinks. Maybe his department chair and assistant principal are right: maybe these guys really *are* assholes. He affects a passive-aggressive head nod in return.

"Hey Peter," Mark says.

"Yeah."

More chuckling.

"Did you just get those shoes?"

"Yeah, why. I mean I got them on sale but . . ."

"I can see that."

"There's no way you can tell."

"Check the bottom of your feet."

Peter hears a chorus of cackling. He sits up and discovers white stickers on each foot announcing original department store prices and deeply discounted savings. Evidently he's overlooked this particular detail. By now sliding under his desk and out of sight seems like a pretty good option. Awash in embarrassment, he searches unsuccessfully for a cover-up.

"That's really funny," Mark says, "let me tell you about my first day on the job."

Peter's mind drifts as Mark begins talking. All morning Peter has been trying to project an aura of confidence and authority. Shirt pressed, slacks creased, loafers shiny new. But he's pretending, making it up as he goes, trying to convince students, teachers, and admin that he's really a teacher. With one question, Mark has uncovered the fraud yet he's also telling Peter something else. He's saying Welcome in. If you can take it and give it back you can hang. Ridicule is the sign of our affection.

Perhaps the immediate lesson is don't wear stickers on your loafers. In some ways, though, everyone does. The stickers are those occasional moments when you reveal to the world you're faking it—that the emperor has no clothes and you really have no idea how to teach. The stickers might reincarnate as typos on a handout, or as a wrong answer to an obscure question during class discussion, or as laundry day in a shared apartment complex with students.

And that's okay. You remove the stickers, edit the misprint, rectify the inaccurate response, and admit it's your t-shirt left in the dryer with a play on words featuring suffrage and Michael Jackson (voting is a thriller), because in the end loafers are still professional footwear, the assignment is clear and well laid out, the Soviets really did control Minsk in 1939 even though Belarus was not entirely independent of the USSR, and if nothing else at least your shirt advocates a noble democratic ideal.

All teachers have sticker moments, of course, but when there is no one with whom to share your insecurities and embarrassments, no one who truly understands what you mean and how you feel, when there is no place to vent or get help, you are more apt to feel lonely and on your own. And like nearly half of all young teachers you are more likely to drop out within your first five years.

This is one reason schools should promote collegiality and collaboration. Poor teacher retention is expensive and inefficient, costing taxpayers many dollars each year training extra recruits while wasting administrative resources hiring extra teachers to replace those who needlessly burn out.

In order to lessen turnover, faculties should be welcoming and supportive of young teachers. First- and second-year mentor programs are one solution but require funding unavailable in some cash-strapped districts. Creating an appropriate culture, on the other hand, requires less money but more leadership.

Clearly being friends with colleagues isn't essential but it also doesn't hurt. If you're fortunate you have coworkers willing to share curriculum and lend a supportive ear. On Peter's first day it's impossible to know how utterly misguided were his initial trepidations of the lunchroom. Eventually they will become a great cause of his happiness and resilience as a teacher.

While sitting in a desk wearing stickered loafers, even if his career will be jeopardized by association, from that day forward Peter will eat nowhere else. Hazed but welcomed, he feels part of the lunchroom. Assuming he can learn how to dress.

KEY IDEAS

- Having colleagues with whom to share highs and lows, to commiserate, laugh, and seek advice, is essential.
- As a result, schools should promote collegiality and collaboration, which will also decrease the share of teachers who quit within their first five years due to loneliness and isolation.

Chapter 10

Crop Dusting

Teachers fold into plastic seats, exhaling in a chorus. Tupperware snaps open, revealing homemade sandwiches, salads, and sliced apples. A microwave beeps, radiating vapors of leftover fried rice, steamed sausage, and limp broccoli. Thin sunlight twists through slotted blinds.

Soon the conversation heats up. For some reason, teachers begin discussing which animals a human could defeat in a fight. Ready for a lively discussion, Justin realizes he needs to use the bathroom. But not wanting to miss a moment of lunch he suppresses the urge, amassing a debt he'll soon repay with interest.

"There is no way you could beat a dog."

"Pound for pound humans are the weakest of animals."

"What about a goat?"

"A human-sized goat would be pretty fierce."

"A dolphin!"

The discussion meanders, gains new life, trails off. Bread crusts and orange rinds spread like shrapnel over soiled paper napkins and filmy Ziploc bags. A plastic knife lies between two desks. The minutes speed past.

Moments from the bell, Justin pivots toward his classroom. The urge has returned but now it's too late. Having twice delivered this lesson, once when it's fresh and again for fine-tuning, he switches to autopilot: intro, insert joke, roll out activity, check for understanding. He sneaks a final sip from his metal canteen.

After he overviews the agenda and answers a few questions, Justin feels a gaseous rumble in his bowels. His stomach feels like an Alhambra water cooler, bubbles glugging toward the surface. He starts facilitating a class discussion but his attention is elsewhere, drawn toward a netherworld of gastric animus.

Soon Justin transitions and directs students to form small groups examining different philosophers of the Industrial Revolution. Thankfully, the work is now student-centered so he can relax and guide as needed, save precious energy just in case. But as he sits at his desk a sharp pain lances across his lower abdomen, jerking him sideways while straightening his spine. He clenches his buttocks to delay the inevitable. It's going to be a long, uncomfortable class.

Pinballing between groups, he makes sure the Jeremy Benthams and John Stuart Millses are clearly articulating utilitarian doctrine, that the Robert Owenses are sufficiently utopian, the Karl Marxes adequately proletariat. Hearing a question from across the room he doesn't wait for an answer, walking instead toward a confused table of communists.

Then suddenly, without warning, he feels his posterior release a puff of gas. Like a toreador he instinctively pirouettes, leaving behind an invisible cloud of malodorous dust. In seconds he's sure the immediate area will begin to smell so he ambles toward the Jane Adamses at the opposite end of class, along the way crop dusting the utilitarians and the communists, a sharp fragrance lingering in his wake.

"Aw who *farted*, man?"

"It was Tyler. You stink!"

"Wasn't me," Tyler says.

"Eww, come on, man."

This is social homicide. Justin's flatulence is killing poor Tyler, a lovely sophomore still discovering the mysteries of hair gel and denim. Tyler desperately wants to fit in, but it seems Justin has just made that more difficult.

"What's going on, guys?" Justin looks over as if puzzled, now safely separated from the incriminating fumes. He considers calling a campus supervisor to cover his class. But there are only three campus sups and the faculty numbers over eighty, so if a mere 4 percent of teachers need to use the bathroom simultaneously, well, you guessed it: he's . . . out of luck. And though Justin is in a pinch he realizes he'll just have to suck it up.

Justin explains the next activity, in which students now join mixed-philosopher groups, and once again the class is humming independently. *You can do it*, he thinks, clenching for good measure, *just thirty more minutes. Hang in there.*

Fortunately, the philosophical roundtable is entertaining and time passes quickly. After debriefing as a class students begin to pack up and evacuate. They cannot leave soon enough, and soon Justin is sitting at last in porcelain repose (Rodin's true inspiration, a high schooler might note).

However scatological, Justin's plight illustrates how education is the rare occupation in which one cannot use the bathroom when desired. Like Justin, teachers must maintain four to five hours of daily bowel regulation, week-to-week, month-to-month, spread over years in the classroom.

Indeed, students are not all one must learn to control. That teachers have clearly defined windows of relief is somewhat unique among the professions. Doctors aren't always in surgery, lawyers not always in court, police not always conducting arrests, firefighters not always dousing flames, nurses not always treating emergencies, businesspeople not always doing uninterruptable business-related things; in fact, it is difficult to imagine another career as consistently constrained.

Though crop dusting students might seem like a ridiculous subject, it suggests teachers are human. They're people with regular needs who occasionally endure mild unpleasantries—at least for several ninety-minute periods each day—in order to educate a community. And they know it's a worthy sacrifice.

Here's how it works. When lunch arrives you gather for a breath of adult distraction. This often involves silly banter, like what animals one could defeat in a fight, which can leave you with less time for other important obligations. Because forget doing your business under the pressure of a ten-minute morning break—that's when disaster strikes. You've got lunch, plus your prep period.

So plan your meals and your bathroom visits accordingly, and plan on farting in class.

KEY IDEAS

- Teachers are only able to use the restroom for brief moments throughout the day.
- This can cause discomfort and create precarious situations in the classroom.

Chapter 11

That's What Mentors Are For

Aristotle and Socrates, Bob Dylan and Woody Guthrie, Luke Skywalker and Obi-Wan: every great pupil requires a great mentor. Even ordinary folks hoping to be slightly above average need mentors too. Everyone does.

Tim meets his in a portable on the outskirts of a high-school campus. She possesses all the accolades: National Board certification, board member for an international project-based learning nonprofit, part-time college instructor and full-time teacher.

He walks into Shannon's classroom on a Thursday afternoon wearing mesh shorts and a reversible mesh basketball jersey. His rec league is directly after class and he figures there'll be little time to change before the game. It's the second semester of Tim's one-year teacher credentialing program, and just before Thanksgiving he's been hired at another school in the district, as an intern to relieve a pregnant teacher.

Tim is so impressed with Shannon that most days after class he lingers, hoping to collect a few extra tips like a squirrel gathering nuts for winter. The next year a full-time position opens at Shannon's school and when Tim is hired she becomes his official mentor in her formal capacity as one of two mentors school-wide, and also unofficially as a department member with whom Tim has already developed a relationship.

When you're a young teacher, "What are the kids doing tomorrow?" is an all-consuming question. The only question there is. And Shannon has helped Tim and his credentialing classmates answer it. She shows them a number of concrete, discipline-specific instructional methods. Here's a project idea, she'll say; This is a technique for group presentations; Here's a note-taking strategy for homework; Consider this template for setting up a gradebook.

In contrast to other more theoretical courses, Shannon's provides the tools. She helps them piece together the puzzle of their upcoming lesson plans.

Tim is Dorothy in his own fantasy world—*Teacherland*—and Shannon is his Good Witch of the North.

Over the summer Shannon gives Tim an electronic copy of all her files. Use what you like, she says, you'll undoubtedly develop stuff that's better. In truth Tim borrows most of it. Without question the jewel in the crown is Shannon's course calendar. Featuring a lesson for each class of the semester, it's a template for success, the cipher to a world of previously unlocked knowledge, his very own Rosetta stone of pedagogy.

As an intern the year prior Tim had walked head down, trying to focus on the lesson directly in front of him, from period-to-period and day-to-day, just hoping to survive. Now he can look out toward the horizon and envision classes weeks and even months ahead. He even imagines gazing down the path of his own career. But these lofty contemplations will have to wait. "What are you doing tomorrow?" is a relentless, unyielding question demanding his full and constant attention.

Thankfully, Shannon has given him a clue. Lesson planning will be hieroglyphics no longer: Tim now holds the key. Shannon and Tim meet weekly in her room to debrief his progress, during which time he asks questions about the curriculum he's been stealing. Shannon is a saint throughout. She goes above and beyond her official one-period release to make sure Tim is happy and teaching at least fairly well.

Tim is fortunate his district offers a formalized program for first- and second-year teachers, which is secret number one to a school's success. In order to build an expert faculty, it certainly helps offering attractive salaries to recruit better talent, but no matter how promising a beginner, without help they will lose ground to less-qualified peers in other districts who receive additional support. You can be the best recruiter in the world, but without coaching your players will undoubtedly fall behind their competition.

Tim's is a big-market school district blessed with the resources to pay veteran teachers to mentor their rookie peers. Though many of his colleagues are helpful, share curriculum, and lend a sympathetic ear, benevolence does not a successful system make. Institutionalizing goodwill through a mentor program, on the other hand, is an important way for schools to support their younger teachers, which ultimately helps maximize students learning.

The next year, Shannon is Tim's formal mentor once again. They continue to meet every few weeks but the discussions have grown more elevated. Tim wants to address larger themes like power and justice rather than simply covering an assemblage of facts, and to incorporate skills like public speaking and persuasive writing. He wonders if there are better ways to help struggling students.

As a new teacher bubbling with ideas—many of them not very good— he talks and talks and talks while Shannon listens, nudging him in the appropriate direction. She watches him teach and invites him to observe her classes as well. Tim witnesses someone charismatic and in control, whose kids are attentive but not afraid, relaxed and ready to learn.

The years pass and by now Shannon and Tim have been colleagues for some time. Her planning calendar still reverberates through his though its echoes have grown more faint. And from time to time he still asks for her advice. They've grown into true friends, equals. And like all good mentees, he's tried to embody the lessons of his teacher while integrating ideals and ideas of his own.

Shannon has taught Tim how to conquer a ninety-minute block period and she's shown him what it means to make their discipline fun. She's instilled in him the importance of rigor and a belief in fairness for all students. Unlike other great disciples, Tim may not further expand humanity's understanding of existence, record a smash hit, or save the galaxy from evil. But like them, he holds his mentor in high regard, grateful for her service, and he aspires to be the best pupil he can be.

One day Tim asks Shannon if she's ever had a mentor of her own. Oh of course, she says, and explains he taught for many years at a high school not so far away. Shannon speaks of her mentor the way Tim feels about her. Maybe one day, Tim thinks, he'll be lucky enough to continue the tradition.

KEY IDEAS

- Mentors help young teachers improve.
- Schools should adopt formalized mentor programs, and encourage informal peer mentoring, which will increase the efficacy of the entire faculty.

Chapter 12

The Weight

You are a horrible teacher. Your work is futile and inane. The kids' expressions are right: this is pointless. No one remembers anything from high school anyway.

Do they really need to know about the Tennis Court Oath or the spinning jenny or the Second Battle of the Marne or the Wannsee Conference or the Rivonia Trial? Will they remember a thing about it ten years, months, or weeks down the line? How about ten days? How about you give the kids the exact same test the very next day and watch all those crammed facts dissipate from their minds like steam off a rolling boil? Let's be real honest here—you're a teacher and you're not teaching anything.

How did you get into this career in the first place? you think to yourself. You were months shy of entering medical school but withdrew to follow the quixotic path of adolescent education. What a mistake. Now you're years in and can't shake the too-well-known statistic that nearly half of all teachers quit within their first five years. But don't get histrionic. Grow up. You're not thinking of quitting, if you're truthful with yourself, you're just kind of pissed. Maybe this is some lingering frustration or a temporary flare-up.

You're feeling bad but do you really have an idea if you're any good? No one comes by to watch you teach. Even your friends' positive opinions of your work are circumstantial at best. You could be the greatest teacher or the worst and you'd have no idea. So when the kids are flat and unenthusiastic and you're slowly deflating like a leaky hot air balloon—always full of hot air—it can be hard to perk back up and rise again.

Especially early Monday following a mediocre week. You've had a fitful night's sleep and awoken to a sense of anguish. You carry it to work, ziplocked along with your trail mix and tuna sandwich, and the kids see through it and the morning is a grind. Not chaotic because after several years of

55

teaching, classroom management isn't really the issue. Usually the kids are quiet. But sealed lips and zombie eyes suck the life from a room.

You think you've been clear, upbeat, and reasonably engaging. The past two times you introduced European imperialism in previous years it went great. Then the first few periods unfold like silent battles in a Civic War, each class tearing your teacher–student relationships further and further apart. You win some, lose some, and once actually raise your voice in a tone approaching anger, which you haven't done in ages. It works and the room falls quiet and for the moment you prevail, but you know the victory is Pyrrhic.

This time, the final class, you think, will be different. You've hooked them with a provocative tale of liberation and oppression, distributed an intelligible handout to which you made a few slight changes during break. Having set the table you now unveil the enticing feast.

But even though it's time to eat, no one is hungry. You're ringing the triangle—y'all come and get it!—yet there's little interest in what you have prepared. So they sit at their tables and move food around. Slide peas under mashed potatoes, take a few bites of meatloaf, drop some on the floor. No one is leaving until they clear their plate! you want to yell. We'll be here all night if we have to! So gulp it down whether you like it or not.

It's draining and it really doesn't matter. History is trivial; high school is meaningless; who cares. Do most people look back on the curriculum and instruction of their younger lives with nostalgia or a sense of gratitude? Does one remember a thing from their secondary education? Not his or her best friend or first love or last prom or big win or great mistake. You're talking about the ideas, the learning, the sense of wonder.

That's what you're thinking as the bell rings and students begin to leave. Your silently condemned lesson has finally come to a close. Their bags are already packed and it's amazing how quickly they leave against the lugubriousness of their arrival.

"Thank you!" says May.

You look up from behind the fortress of your computer to which you have retreated, certain you're either hearing things or becoming schizophrenic. The sounds register first. You assign them to letters, then shape letters into words and words into meaning. *Thank you.*

"Today was really interesting," she adds.

Her words wash over you slowly, seeping in like a summer rain through cracked earth, replenishing a barren wellspring of emotion. You sit up a little straighter, feel the tension release from your neck. Blood flows to the tips of your fingers and toes. Light shines through the window and onto your face.

"Oh thanks, May. Nice job today."

"Thanks. See you tomorrow!"

You notice your pulse and breathe deeply. Your heart swells; it grows larger and larger and bursts from your chest, drifting out the window and into the cerulean sky. You're not ready to admit it but a teenager has validated your existence—and it feels good.

That's why you do this, you remember, because you like people. And you particularly enjoy the presence of teenagers because they are prickly and cantankerous and flippant and awkward and brimming with life and sincere and amazingly human. You like making people feel good and sharing with them something valuable. Knowledge, the practical and the abstract, the trough, the fishing pole, the means and the end.

You feel light. You step out from behind your desk and smile at the last remaining students. As they leave you float into the halls and toward your friends in their neighboring rooms, hovering. And you know what the poet meant when he wrote hope springs eternal in the human breast. Because today at least, teaching isn't all that bad. The weight has been lifted.

KEY IDEAS

- Putting one's heart and soul into a lesson that receives dismal feedback can feel demoralizing.
- Students have a big effect on teachers' happiness, whether or not teachers would like to admit it.

Chapter 13

Happy Hour

One particular spring evening Nick leaves the high school at which he teaches and goes downtown to meet some buddies after work. The air is warm, almost tropical, the previous months' biting winds now replaced by a lazy breeze.

Approaching the bar he encounters people in good spirits and snappy threads. In the foreground stand his buddies in pro forma casual Friday attire, clutching drinks and chatting in a circle like so many high-school underclassmen. Wearing jeans, canvas shoes, and a slightly wrinkled button-up, Nick does not blend.

His group of friends includes a commercial realtor, an investment banker, a private equity manager, a corporate lawyer, and an accountant. They pay more in taxes than Nick makes in a year. But their relationships predate their marginal tax rates, and like so many Fridays this is just another night with the boys.

Along with them is someone Nick vaguely recognizes.

"Nick, this is our buddy Teddy from New York. He's a trader visiting for the weekend."

"Nice to meet you."

"Nick's a high school teacher."

Teddy regards Nick inquisitively, almost puzzled, trying to make sense of the public employee standing in front of him.

"Oh!" says Teddy, as if overcompensating for his disappointment.

He forces his cheeks up and mouth open, nearly resembling a smile, then quickly looks away in search of a reply.

". . . Good for you," he manages.

It's an all-too-common response.

"Thanks," Nick says, peeved and somewhat deflated.

Good for *me*? he thinks. What does that mean? Good for me I had the audacity to forgo an upper-middle-class existence? Good for me for becoming a selfless saint? Good for me, like "It's a dirty job but someone's gotta do it"; good for me to sacrifice my self-interest for our society. Not good for me teaching is an impressive accomplishment, or good for me I just passed the bar or my National Boards or Series 7. Good for me because Teddy never would have made such an outlandish decision.

"Good for you" is a platitude reserved for those unworthy of genuine admiration. Good for you—because if you're in the classroom you certainly can't do anything else. Perhaps that's how Teddy considers teachers. Lather that warm pat of condescension on someone else's bread, Nick thinks. I'll butter my own.

Or maybe Teddy really does mean Good for you. Maybe he knows it isn't easy to give up money and respect for one's beliefs, and is impressed Nick has made a difficult choice. Good for you, he may have meant to say, follow your heart. It's a noble calling.

Warranted or not, when introduced to friends-of-friends or while pitching woo to single women, this isn't the first time Nick has experienced feelings of professional inadequacy. Perhaps he's projecting, feeling insecure and oversensitive, but the comment is bothersome: he's heard it much too often. Either way, the dilemma shouldn't exist. Altruism is not the only foundation on which to build an economy or a profession.

Like Rodney Dangerfield said, teachers don't get no respect. People are quick to espouse their virtues but in truth the job is considered neither sexy nor elite. Some don't believe it's a true profession at all. Stemming from comparatively low pay and mild barriers to entry, and an imprecise understanding of what teachers actually do, this lack of respect is not entirely unwarranted, but it's most certainly bad for both the career and the country.

Let's be serious. In your heart-of-hearts do you truly consider teaching a demanding, top-tier field tantamount to law, medicine, science, or finance? You don't have to say it—everyone knows the answer. But teaching *should* be considered a desirable occupation for the best and brightest. Top-flight candidates would most certainly create a first-class teaching corps. If the job isn't sufficiently attractive, well, the system needs to change.

How? Easy: more compensation, competition, and understanding. Better remuneration is needed because, for better or worse, skilled and ambitious people often enjoy making money, and teachers shouldn't have to be selfless. Better compensation attracts better talent—that's just the way of the world. More demanding barriers to entry and a more rigorous certification process like the Boards or the bar are also needed so candidates struggle to enter the field and feel a greater sense of accomplishment once there.

And when teachers demonstrate mastery they should be allowed to instruct according to expert standards—just like in medicine, law, and finance. If teaching is seen as exclusive, with formidable barriers to entry, it will become a more respected career, and teachers will earn the right and the latitude to practice. Perhaps most of all, greater understanding is needed so that in the future the profession will be seen as more attractive—à la the Finnish model—and promising candidates will not be deterred from joining it.

Someday, they might even get more respect at the bar.

"We donate to a few charter schools each year," Teddy continues in a well-meaning manner.

As soon as socially acceptable, Teddy ends their conversation and returns to the banter of the group. Social hierarchy established, Nick hurries along and fetches a beer.

Walking to the bar, he orders a pilsner and reflects on his circumstances. Growing up, he never considers becoming a teacher. In his eyes, the profession is neither well-paying nor prestigious. Like laying up or cashing out, teaching is something you do for the lifestyle or because you lack ambition. It leads to hollow clichés and feigned expressions of interest—not the sort of bar banter he desires. All Nick really wants, like so many others, is to stand among friends and feel respected.

After college, Nick begins substitute teaching while studying for graduate school entrance exams. Though he takes a couple, applies, and is accepted to several schools, he senses a growing fear he'll be living from the outside in rather than the inside out. He feels anxious about climbing the ladder of success only to realize it's placed against the wrong wall. The *idea* of it all seems appealing, but in sober moments of reflection Nick questions finding joy and meaning in the trajectory of his future career.

In the end, he chooses to stay in the classroom. Regardless of the societal gap in respect, he decides, he wants to be happy.

The bartender is looking at Nick with impatience, his pilsner warming on the counter.

"Sorry, here you go."

After settling up he notices his investor-buddy, TJ, talking with two women across the bar. TJ smiles and with a subtle up-nod invites Nick to join, but he isn't prepared for more disdain—this time from accomplished members of the opposite sex. Oh, you're a schoolteacher, that's sweet, they will exclaim flatly, their eyes scanning the room, shoulders rounding inward. Good for you. No thanks, Nick thinks, not tonight.

So instead he returns to Teddy and his buddies standing on the patio beneath a darkening sky. They rehash old stories, argue about politics and where to eat dinner. For Nick it's treasured conversation. And eventually, as the night grows dark and the jokes more daft, his feelings of inadequacy recede into the warmth of laughter and too much beer.

KEY IDEAS

- Never say to a teacher, "Good for you."
- The profession would be improved if teachers were better respected, which can be accomplished through more compensation, competition, and understanding.

Chapter 14

Chocolate Walking Tour

There's a story of a high-school science teacher who founds a gourmet chocolate walking tour. She's soft-spoken and gentle and by all accounts adept in the classroom.

One day the science teacher, whom we'll call Rebecca, informs her friends she's developing a side project. The surrounding city is oozing with amazing confections, she says, and she wants to delight the uninitiated with her local gastronomic knowledge. Since the city is famously foot-friendly and, in spite of the intermittent hill, fairly easy to navigate, why not combine the two? People like to walk and they love to eat chocolate. Like hot milk and cocoa, it will be a heavenly match.

Though intriguing, her scheme registers little more than polite if encouraging reactions from her friends, in part because teachers have similarly romantic notions all the time. But by the end of the school year she's gone.

Several months later, Rebecca and her new business are splashed above the nameplate of her local newspaper. She has fulfilled the ultimate teacher-fantasy, pulled the ripcord, ejected from the classroom, and landed on sweeter soil. Rather than instruct adolescents on the intricacies of oceanic subduction zones, she will now educate ambulatory epicures in the chocolate arts. One can imagine her traversing the city with a reusable water bottle and macaroon flag, prodding hungry supplicants toward their next delectable destination.

With July and August and several other weeks scattered throughout the year, teachers have some time for other endeavors. Sometimes they're mere hobbies, other times labors of love; occasionally semi-serious ventures become veritable careers. When Rebecca unveils her idea it's understandable why her colleagues are a little wary. It's normal for teachers to dream of an alternate livelihood—like becoming a screenwriter or opening a bottle shop—but usually the dreams remain just that.

Many people outside teaching undoubtedly ponder different professions as well. It seems intrinsic to the human condition. What's less well understood, though, is why it's so difficult for teachers to actually pull the trigger once they've been in the classroom for a while (spoiler: it's the money).

Most do not leave seeking greater meaning; many who exit early do so from loneliness and isolation. Once they hit a certain mark, however, teachers find the Golden Handcuffs difficult to escape, like hares inching toward the financial finish line of their careers.

In Teacherland it's called Step and Column since most public school districts base compensation off a salary schedule. There are two ways for teachers to earn more money: either acquire more education, like continuing credits or an advanced degree, or simply complete another year of teaching. The salary schedule is a giant grid with years taught and education earned on the y- and x-axes, respectively. If it's your first year teaching and you have the minimum level of education, you begin in the upper left-hand corner.

An increase in units or degrees earned moves you one column to the right while an increase in years taught moves you one step down (which is really a step up). Hence Step and Column. Eventually you reach the bottom right of the matrix where you have maxed out and the taste is bittersweet—like a dark chocolate—because although you're making the most money you have also hit your financial ceiling. All you can hope for is a stipend for taking on a leadership role or coaching position, or a raise through collective bargaining.[1]

So why the Golden Handcuffs? If you're thinking of switching districts and teaching somewhere else, most schools will offer you a few years down—or up—the scale. But hacking years off your step placement often means taking a significant pay cut, which is a disincentive for leaving the district and shackles teachers to their current gig.

Even if you work at a great school and have no plans to move, it's still nice to imagine the possibility. Ironically, if it were simpler to come and go more people might take a few years off and jump back in. And if it became easier to leave, some people sticking around for the paycheck might realize they're better suited for something else, and actually have the means to do it.

The Golden Handcuffs present another unfairness too. Unlike most employees who pay into Social Security, teachers contribute to a pension pool instead. This is fine if they remain in public education their entire career but if they'd like to do something else, like open a bottle shop, become a screenwriter, or begin a chocolate walking tour, they collect only a small retirement from the teacher pool and a small retirement, if any, from Social Security. (The same is true of government employees at large in a number of states.)

Plus if one's spouse has been a teacher and the primary breadwinner, he or she receives less survivor benefits than in the private sector. This has to do with the Government Pension Offset and the Windfall Elimination Provision and some other laws written by Congress in the 1970s, but the larger point is one of systemic inequity. The original rationale was to prevent spouses, and employees themselves, from "double dipping," though in practice it's more like "double stiffing" because of the reduced benefits. In the private sector, on the other hand, one can get Social Security and a company pension, no problem.

So while Rebecca was able to break free from the Golden Handcuffs because of the success of her urban cocoa safari, others won't be so fortunate. What would you do? If you're ten or twenty years into your career, if you've finally reached a respectable salary, there's a strong chance you'll fear giving it up. It's true teaching jobs exist everywhere, but if you leave the profession and want to return your income will likely be halved. And then there's the question of retirement.

So sure, you could escape, but freedom isn't always free. Sometimes it's quite expensive—especially if you're uncertain you can afford it. Or you could just take the leap, take a walk, and start discovering your local chocolates.

KEY IDEA

• Compensation structures in education reward longevity which, though teachers often fantasize about it, makes leaving the profession difficult to do.

NOTE

1. Your union can either negotiate a straight raise by adding a flat percentage to the entire chart, or a percentage off the chart in the form of a one-time bonus; or you can negotiate more steps and columns. And whether or not teachers should be paid according to experience and education, as opposed to student test scores à la merit-based pay, for example, is a matter of some national debate. But the current system is largely workable, in part because public schoolteachers are public employees and many public employees are similarly remunerated.

Chapter 15

I'm Here to Teach

It's time to eat. And evidently, to make some music. Walking into his customary lunchroom, Chad encounters a temporary recording studio. Mario has set up a microphone and stand and is fiddling with newly installed recording software on a laptop behind the desk.

"Chad, you ready?"

"For what?" he says, nervous and stalling.

"To rap."

"I have my lyrics—let's do this!" interrupts Jeremy as he enters the room. Jeremy sets down his lunch and picks up the headphones. Launching into his composition he palms the air in front of him, stroking it, moving like a police officer directing traffic. After several takes Jeremy is satisfied and sits down.

"Okay, Chad, you're up."

Chad leaves his unopened lunch on a desk and walks to the front of the room. Sliding the headphones over his ears he hears a canned drumbeat, distorted guitar riff, and synthesized baseline reminiscent of the late-1980s. He waits for the right timing, like a game of double dutch, catches the beat and jumps in.

Several days later the song is unveiled for everyone at lunch. To the verses Mario has appended his own, stitching them together with the track's hook, also its title, in which he shouts *"I'M HERE TO TEEEEACH!"* as if purging himself of some atavistic truth. The room laughs and applauds and celebrates the absurdity of their creation.

Though you may think otherwise, behind this frivolity lies a deeper truth. In one respect, the song is merely a colorful example of teachers recharging between classes. You get ten to fifteen minutes in the morning and again in the afternoon, plus thirty to forty-five minutes for lunch, so when congregating away from teenagers it's natural to crave some release.

Yet their song also shows how teachers assume the characteristics of their students. (One need look no further than afternoon staff meetings.) Teachers graft youthful traits onto their own personalities because they are what teachers know, what teachers encounter most hours of most working days.

If only subconsciously, Mario, Chad, and Jeremy were rapping to better understand their students. Because being able to relate to them is a foundational skill. It's as important to know who you are as a person, and who you were as a teen, as it is to stay abreast of cultural trends.

The three may also have been attempting to stay relevant. It's why teachers sign up for the latest social network, download the newest apps, why from time to time they feel compelled to watch reality television, even if they don't want to do any of these things. One needs to know the argot and the styles of the moment because it will aid in becoming a better teacher. Of course, as teachers age this is no simple feat. Eventually they become their parents, and keeping current gets harder and harder to accomplish.

In the end, however, maybe it's much more simple. Maybe Mario, Chad, and Jeremy were simply trying to remain young. If they feel young, they teach young. Sometimes it's necessary to act like students in order to understand them, and sometimes this means rapping in a classroom at lunch.

After all, they're here to teach.

KEY IDEA

• It's important for teachers to relate to students; and sometimes this means acting silly.

Chapter 16

The Flip Out

Steve is already late to the party. As a relatively new teacher, he's not as efficient finalizing grades as everyone else, and they've started without him. Unlatching the wooden side gate, he steps onto a brick footpath lined with ivy and coolers of beer and hears classic rock spilling from portable speakers. Walking into the narrow backyard, he encounters a pack of jubilant teachers scattered across a wooden deck, behind a young maple tree, and around a charcoal Weber grill.

One teacher is sitting in spandex shorts under a canopy of oak trees, riding shirt unzipped to his belly button exposing a tuft of curly, black hair. Nearby another is holding a tall bottle of beer, locked in deep conversation. Others are standing in the shade, chatting on benches, lounging in plastic chairs.

Steve moves from one group to another saying hello, and at the soonest acceptable moment absconds to fix a plate of food. Before he can finish eating, however, his friend drags him into the music room past a diverse collection of guitars.

"Where were you?" she says. "I've been waiting to open this."

She shows him a box that, she whispers, contains the party accessories they have designed. They slit the packaging tape, peel back the cardboard flaps, and struggle to contain their excitement: green mesh trucker caps are embossed with a My Little Pony–inspired unicorn jumping over a rainbow and the words "Don't Stop Believin' in the Lunchroom." They shove the hats in the box and hurry back outside.

"Do you know what time it is?"

Steve's friend calls everyone to the deck.

"Are you guys ready for some *flair*?" She leans down, removes a trucker cap, and places it on her head. "Then come and get 'em!"

Teachers rush the cardboard box like free coffee in a break room.

When the hats are distributed, everyone makes for the roof. By working the angles just right it's possible to maneuver up the sidewall and over the gutters. After ascending, lying on their backs in liberation, they talk about the year, share victories big and small, tell stories about parents, students, and admin as if this were an exorcism, a group therapy session, a collective catharsis. On this the first day of summer they will begin the healing process, the first step in preparing for the following year.

Steve is basking on the roof in the glory of the moment and the world feels right. Even if in the eyes of others they're acting so wrong. Teachers aren't supposed to behave this way but many of them do; they know how necessary it is to celebrate the end of a school year. For the Lunchroom, the teachers with whom Steve eats most days at school, this party is an annual tradition. Win, lose, or draw.

Like the end of a season, you rejoice. You toast the good times and the bad, the successful new lessons and those that failed, the father with whom you'll no longer have to communicate and the mother whom you've enjoyed getting to know, the students you're glad to be rid of and the ones you're sad to see walk out your door.

Summer break is indeed an interesting concept. What some consider time to refresh, recharge, and reconnect, others feel is vestigial, preindustrial, obsolete. If one may be permitted to paraphrase Nietzsche: the utility of a thing is not necessarily derived from its origin. In other words, just because summer is rooted in an agricultural past, and the country is now a modern society, this doesn't mean "vacation" is no longer of use. Like an off-season in the sporting world, breaks are an important part of performing at peak level.

And while the mind may require less rest than the body it may nonetheless benefit from an annual shift in perspective. For teachers this might mean reading Tolstoy on the beach and reimagining your curriculum, or songwriting in the music room of your bungalow and finding inspiration to create a documentary film academy with your colleagues. For students, while they might lose ground if they're not thinking throughout June, July, and August, these months are also a time to learn for its own sake, experientially, to travel, labor, and read.

Steve and his friends are sprawled on the roof with their green mesh trucker hats when the wind picks up and the sun dips down behind a neighboring ridge. Stars begin to punctuate the sky.

"I'm out of beer," a voice calls through the crepuscule.

They descend and gather on the weathered deck. Then someone appears with a bottle of tequila, signaling the awards ceremony is about to begin.

A menu-sized stone tablet is revealed etched with the words *A teacher Takes a hand, Opens a mind, Touches a heart, Shapes the future.* It was once given to a member of the Lunchroom by a parent, and ever since has become a sardonic honor bestowed upon a different teacher every June.

But this year is slightly different. The recipient, Betty, will be retiring early after almost a decade in the classroom. She's told that while her decision to leave the profession is understandable, she's a good teacher and will be missed. Betty begins to cry and they smother her with hugs.

"So now is it tequila time?" someone says breaking the silence.

They agree indeed it is. Several people go inside to crank the music and line up shots while those outside start to dance, singing, stomping, bowing the loose boards of the deck.

The night will continue in this fashion until some time later—several minutes or several hours, it's difficult to tell through the haze of leftovers and beer—when a heavy knock sounds at the front door and a flashlight beams in through the window.

"Cops!"

"Shit!"

"*Shhhhh.*"

Like so many high schoolers they kill the music and the conversation and wait for someone in charge to go outside. Fortunately the cops are cool. They kindly ask everyone to keep it down, explaining they're getting noise complaints, and soon depart without incident.

Eventually teachers begin to leave too. Several walk home, a few others ride their bikes, and someone calls a cab. With the crowd thinning, Steve and the remainders attempt strumming guitars in the living room—only most are in no condition to play. One falls asleep on the floor, at the foot of another teacher sleeping in an oversize chair.

This is a unique group of coworkers who feel so comfortable together, so at ease with one another. In teaching it's important to be vulnerable and though partying with colleagues isn't a requirement, it certainly helps approach public education with a sense of wonderment, pleasure, and awe.

Late the next morning, Steve awakes to a sense of euphoria and a tall stack of pancakes. Outside the sun is shining and the trees are green. The Lunchroom has feted another school year, another season of teaching and learning. They have flipped out. And in Teacherland, summer has now begun.

KEY IDEAS

- The end of a school year is like the end of a sports season; and win, lose, or draw, it merits a celebration.
- Summer break serves an important function for teachers and students alike: to learn and experience outside the confines of the classroom.
- Performing at peak level often requires rest, which summer break provides.

Section III

THE ART AND CRAFT PART II

Chapter 17

The Dandelion of Judah

"What's a diaspora?" a student asks.

Linda is searching for an appropriate response, unsure quite how to answer. "Does anybody know?"

Across the room she sees a canvas of blank stares, no color or light. The discussion has been rolling along nicely and the question is fair—necessary vocabulary for understanding the Israeli–Palestinian conflict they've been studying in class. Linda has assigned a chapter of a book as supplemental reading but unfortunately its vocabulary is proving a little too ornate. She's already fielded questions about the meaning of reparations and repatriation.

"Okay, no one? It's like a spreading out of people."

She registers a few head nods but for most the concept is still unclear.

"You know, when people spread out from some initial place."

Rephrasing her first explanation doesn't really help. Linda feels a collective shuffling of bodies and senses students' eagerness to move on. She could ask for a show of fingers one-through-five or a thumbs-up-thumbs-down as quick checks for understanding, but both techniques seems elementary-esque.

They've been analyzing the four main components of the conflict—Jerusalem, borders, Israeli security, Palestinian refugees—and trying to understand how two peoples could claim ownership over the same piece of land, especially when one hasn't lived there for a really long time. Kelly, an inquisitive freshman, doesn't understand the meaning of "the Jewish diaspora," a phrase from the book.

"So were the Palestinian refugees who fled during the war a diaspora too?" she asks.

"You mean is there a Palestinian diaspora? Well not all people who get kicked out of their homes turn into a diaspora. It's like—"

Linda needs to change course. She could call up the Oxford or Merriam-Webster definitions, talk about big-D Diaspora officially describing Jews residing outside Israel and small-d diaspora referring to people in general who've been scattered from their original homeland—African, Persian, Irish—or even break down the Greek etymological roots of diaspora as *diaspeirein* meaning to disperse, which appears in the Septuagint version of the Bible in Deuteronomy chapter 28. All much too bland. She needs a new angle.

"It's like when you blow on the weed with the green stem and the ball of dusty white pollen discharges like a firework. *Ffwwwoooooo*." She opens her arms out wide, palms unfurled, pantomiming the action.

"A dandelion!"

"No, a dandelion is that pretty yellow wildflower with all the petals."

"They're the same thing!" says Kelly.

The class erupts. Some students gang up on Linda while others have her back. A few look about bewilderedly or begin playing on their phones. The lesson is spinning out of control, on that exciting precipice of mayhem. Linda is about to climb atop the verbal heap and reassert her authority when Carlos pulls everyone together.

He wades in below the shouting. "Look, " Carlos says softly. He's showing Linda a big yellow flower on the screen of his smartphone. "It's a video, watch."

Students in his area crowd around but Linda is hesitant to follow. Using phones in class is technically a violation of school policy. Though it's necessary to guard against abuse it seems Carlos is making connections, learning not messing around, so Linda lets it slide. After a brief pause she circles behind him as other students take out their phones and search for similar clips.

On Carlos's small rectangular display is a time-lapse video of a dandelion—French for "tooth of a lion" (*dent de lion*), she learns, which reminds her of the Lion of Judah, emblem of the Hebrew tribe, but she puts that aside. Beginning as a forest-green lollipop it opens to unveil a splendor of golden pedals shining proud and bright. Then the flower begins the same process in reverse.

It curls over itself behind a wall of protective leaves; and there it stands, dormant, like a lollipop once more. Inside, the yellow interior pedals age and lose their color. Seconds later, the leaves unfold again, revealing a round, white puff like the hair of an eccentric professor. Finally the spores float away, fleeing their roots to scatter miles across the globe—a botanical exodus.

"Told you," says Kelly.

"That's fascinating," replies Linda.

Then she tries to get everyone back on track.

"Okay, the Diaspora. Someone connect the dots for us. Why have we been looking up dandelion videos on our phones?"

This, here, is the moment of truth. No lightbulbs or flashes of recognition and their little detour has been a waste. Fortunately several hands shoot into the air.

"Daniel."

"Well a dandelion's pollen starts on the stem then spreads all over—just like the Jews started in Israel and spread all over the world."

"Bingo—nice, Daniel. Everyone get his point?"

At last Linda sees expressions of understanding on students' faces. It's been a brief digression but in her estimation a valuable one. Was it worth ten minutes to delve into the meaning of the word "diaspora," a minor point in the grand scheme of the lesson and the class? In her judgment, yes it was. Part of teaching is knowing when and for how long to get lost in the tributaries of some larger stream of thought. The real art, though, involves *how* to explain an idea. How to sync with the wavelengths of the teenage mind.

In the absence of a pop culture reference Linda tried metaphor, using imagery to animate an abstraction. Fireworks, the white hair of an eccentric professor, a dandelion: association is a powerful apparatus of the mind, and knowing when and how to use it is an important teaching tool.

Overuse of imagery and metaphor can be counterproductive, of course, even reductive, but therein lies the art. Metaphor is but one of many possible ways to bring an idea to life, which teachers try to do every period of every day. And linking in one's mind the spreading out of a people with the seeds of a wildflower is not necessarily a poor way to remember.

"Okay that was fun," Linda says. "Now where were we?"

They finish their discussion in a straightforward manner. When things get heady she interjects a brief story, an anecdote to keep everyone engaged. For the rest of class, students participate in a conflict-resolution simulation before assembling to review the main ideas of the day.

It's time to go but Linda can't resist.

"Now let's see if you can get this last one right," she says. "You know what I'm going to ask. What's a diaspora?"

"A dandelion!" several people shout.

Linda could require someone explain further but the point has been made and she's confident most won't soon forget. For effect she blows on an imaginary wildflower. Several kids wipe pollen from their faces, and one affects a playful sneeze.

"Now what's the Dandelion of Judah?" she asks, largely for her own amusement as students begin to exit.

Like seeds in a slipstream the wordplay sails over their heads, and into the mystic beyond.

KEY IDEAS

- There is a certain art in explaining an idea to students.
- This often involves the use of metaphor, imagery, relevant references, and creative language.

Chapter 18

The Zen of Teaching

They say if you fail to prepare, then prepare to fail. The Internet attributes this chiasmic maxim to Benjamin Franklin, with a slight twist by champion swimmer Mark Spitz. Whatever the axiom's provenance, its advice is relevant to nearly every human endeavor, including teaching.

Teachers have long understood the importance of preparation, but many still wonder about the labeling of their profession as either art or science. While there are concrete strategies, methods, and techniques to master, in its most elemental state teaching is a performance—like arguing for passage of the Declaration of Independence or winning seven gold medals at the 1972 Olympic Summer Games in Munich. Preparation is essential—but it doesn't negate the primacy of executing in the moment.

So when Andre is asked one afternoon to cover his friend's AP European History class the following morning, suffice it to say he's underprepared.

"Sure," he replies. "But what are you doing?"

In his friend Gabe's eyes shines a mischievous twinkle. On his lips, a faint wry smile.

Andre chuckles. "What are you doing in class?" he repeats.

"Your favorite, Hobbes and Locke." Gabe knows Andre finds both men's writings on the nature of man and the social contract enthralling.

"Okay, what do you want me to do?"

"Whatever you'd like," Gabe says. "You've had a lot of these kids before. They're all fairly high level and also pretty cool. I'll leave you the lesson I did with third period today and you can either use it or scrap it—up to you."

That afternoon Andre recalls his stint as a substitute. Mostly improvising, he had never actually been trained how to teach. Each day he'd open an unfamiliar classroom door and pray for a sub plan, on good days leaving him with minutes—and bad days sometimes seconds—to prepare. Nonetheless, ad-libbing in the moment was fun.

This time around Andre has the evening to think about a lesson for the following morning (plus a teaching credential). But he still doesn't know what Gabe has accomplished in third period, or how, so he'll just have to extemporize, improvise, make it up as he goes.

This scenario represents a fundamental tension in teaching: being at once well prepared and in the moment. An overreliance on planning can zap the dynamism from a class, and even the tightest lesson does not always unfurl predictably each time—what works for one group may not work equally well with another.

Much like a stand-up comic's routine varies from show to show depending on the audience, if a teacher relies too heavily on his or her plan and forgets to respond to the individual kids in the room, less learning, like fewer laughs, will undoubtedly result.

Yet while minimal planning might force teachers to be more mentally present because they have nothing else on which to rely, a rudderless class is more likely to sail off course, resulting in mutiny, desertion, a scurvy of the mind. The best practitioners are those who are constantly mindful of striking just the right balance between creating a good lesson and being able to throw it all away.

The next morning Andre arrives early and alights at his desk. After scanning for any explosive emails, he pulls *The Leviathan* and *The Second Treatise on Government* from his bag, flipping through the pages once more like a student perusing her notes before an exam: not so much as review but assurance.

Walking across the hall about five minutes into the period, he enters Gabe's room and is introduced to the class. They greet him with friendly smiles; he recognizes several familiar faces.

"Treat him well, everyone," says Gabe on his way out.

Andre starts chatting with a kid he knows in the front row then spins toward the door. But Gabe has already left. Shuffling about, Andre checks on Gabe's desk, underneath the podium, along the whiteboard, but can't find the lesson plans anywhere. He thinks of asking the students but figures this will lead to uncertainty and lessen his appearance of control.

Oh well, better start, he says to himself, but doesn't know exactly how to proceed. He needs a plan. Finding a video on the Internet or directing students to journal quietly both seem like cop-outs. Then an odd feeling of excitement fills his lungs.

He can just *talk* about a subject in which he's keenly interested with a group of highly intelligent young men and women who aren't even his students. Andre won't be responsible for their achievement, he realizes, and feels strangely liberated to explore some of the most important ideas in Western political thought purely for the sake of learning itself. It might even be fun.

Later Andre is told by a trusted student that the next eighty minutes transpire with a mix of humor, clumsiness, and fitful energy. Andre recalls a sea monster projected against the wall, a flurry of turned pages and impassioned oratories, but that's about it. The student says Andre is "kind of all over the place" running around class and sitting on desks and drawing on the whiteboard, that it's interesting seeing two teachers cover similar material in different ways.

There's a common saying in education that teachers make more decisions in a given day second only to air traffic controllers. Aside from answering questions before and after class, teaching often requires complete focus from bell to bell. You're trying to engage all students all the time, being present for them individually and as a group. Perhaps because of this some teachers tend to plan more than others. Some script lessons down to the minute while others create outlines and follow them loosely.

If you know exactly what you're doing from moment to moment you're less likely to waste time. It's a nod to efficiency. But what happens when a student asks a provocative question and the class is enthused, when you want to descend the rabbit hole, take a detour, discuss the psychology behind Hobbes' premature birth and absentee father or the effects of the English Civil War on his relatively somber view of humanity? And who's to say every group will require the same amount of time to complete an assignment?

If everyone is working hard and one period needs twice as long as the next, why should you cut off the former prematurely? By allowing yourself the flexibility to make decisions in the moment, knowing the effects of these decisions will ripple throughout the semester, you can actually create space for greater learning to occur: the pedagogical equivalent of the butterfly effect.

Teachers are at their finest when they accept the tension between preparing and staying present; between knowing exactly what you want to do beforehand and having the ability to create something completely new in an instant. Some methods of instruction are best when invented on the fly, while others succeed only after weeks of tinkering.

Fail to prepare and prepare to fail, sure enough. But in class if you aren't fully in the moment, despite whatever planning you may have done days, weeks, even years before, then you are also less likely to succeed. Teaching is both art and science, part Buddhist mindfulness, part precision engineering.

So to the adage of the wise Ben Franklin, with an assist from Olympian Mark Spitz, I would add this: if you forget to be present, then your presence will be forgetful.

KEY IDEAS

- A tension exists between preparing for a lesson and being present while teaching it.
- Both are important, yet sometimes teachers overcompensate for one at the expense of the other.

Chapter 19

Why It's Better to Get Diarrhea Than a Sub

When people in other professions want to take a sick day, the procedure is undoubtedly straightforward. They notify their bosses and work either continues or waits until they return. The process is similar for teachers, except regardless of their attendance, students will still be in class and they'll still need something to do. And you can only show so many movies.

Plus if you're going to require anything more demanding of substitutes than pressing play you'll need to tell them explicitly and in detail. Teachers can't just call in sick, they need to prepare for their absence, and sometimes it's easier to tough it out.

Perhaps it's Jason's fault for ordering the seafood soup. Opening an app on his smartphone, he finds a nearby restaurant with four out of five stars and orders a dish he's eaten many times before. It's sweet and sour with just the right level of heat and brimming with shellfish. Devouring it methodically Jason settles into a cocoon of mind-numbing evening television, relaxing before the week ahead.

His troubles begin around midnight. He dreams he's being hunted by a school of ghastly piscine beasts. The slow-motion chase is interminable and when he finally escapes he wakes to a paroxysm of stomach pain. Throwing off the covers he hobbles hurriedly to the bathroom. His forehead heats up, he begins to perspire, and along the sides of his tongue his mouth waters in that visceral precursor to retching. Then he starts retching. And then, he has diarrhea.

In time, both subside and Jason is left with the sweats and a still-achy stomach. Overriding all sensation, however, is the thought he'll not make it to school in the morning. He hopes his illness is fleeting, figures sleep will help and only time will tell. Eventually he returns to bed, drifts off, and is roused by the buzzing of his alarm.

Lifting his head from the pillow in a brief moment of weightlessness he
feels the previous night's symptoms return to his body. He rushes to the
toilet, reaching into a nearby medicine cabinet to find a thermometer and
check his temperature. It's slightly elevated—a bad sign, especially after just
waking up.

At this point there are two options: phone in sick or tough it out. But since
he's never requested a sub without plenty of warning he cannot quite recall
the process. He can attempt remembering the number for Subfinder or find a
link on his school's website. Texting a teacher friend or emailing the principal's secretary are possibilities as well, but if Jason really does have a fever
the responsible play is not going to work.

But if he does stay home his replacement will need to know what to do.
When arranging substitutes Jason usually spends significant time creating a
plan for them to follow. Ideally the sub teaches the same curriculum using
the same methods of instruction; but sometimes a lesson requires too much
background knowledge, too many moving parts, too specific a use of technology. In this case Jason will have to modify his lesson—essentially creating a
throwaway for the time he's gone knowing he'll never use it again.

Rather than creating an intricate plan, Jason's other option is rolling tape.
Just find a video on the Internet or in the school library and his lesson is finished. Students will be thankful he's not making them do work and the sub
will have less to mishandle. If learning weren't his primary objective playing
movies might almost be a win-win.

Either way Jason will need to provide written instructions. He usually
emails his subs detailed lesson plans several days beforehand in case they
have any questions. Though writing these instructions might seem straightforward, it's often a Pandora's box because it's difficult knowing how much
explanation to include. For example, saying, "Discuss last night's reading
with students" won't suffice; you can't expect substitutes to lead a discussion
about something for which they have had minutes to prepare.

Plus if you want students to complete an activity, you may be unsure
whether the sub can sufficiently facilitate it. You're torn between scripting
detailed instructions, which could take pages, and condensing your wishes
into several sentences, which might be clearer but will necessarily omit
important information. It doesn't matter how many typographical tricks you
employ to highlight your instructions—bold, italics, whacky font, red lettering—some will go unnoticed.

If the substitute manages to understand your directions and follow them,
and if students successfully complete their assignments by the end of the
period, you also need to decide whether or not they will turn them in. If students are to keep their papers overnight you'll probably get fewer back upon
your return. Yet if a sub collects them, students always have a trump card to

play: claiming they were never asked to hand anything in. Instead of papers you may return to a pile of excuses. You may figure it's easier not having a sub at all.

So in spite of Jason's illness, he comes to school. He doesn't eat breakfast or pack a lunch. Fortunately classes are only forty-five minutes, which means he'll have to endure less than an hour of bathroom-less instruction at a time. He looks ashen and feels even worse. Perhaps most of all, in this age of social networks and Internet infamy, he fears the horrors a room of teenagers might deliver upon the poor educator who soils himself in front of his class.

Between each of the first four periods Jason spends most of his time squatting safely in the teachers' restroom, and somehow he survives until lunch. Ordinarily he eats with friends down the hall but instead he dims the lights and lies beneath the lee of his bulky desk. Somehow he wakes up feeling rejuvenated, approaching normalcy for the first time in nearly twelve hours. He thinks about finding something to eat but decides against it, knowing he can leave early since his last period of the day is a prep.

Soon he's in bed where his misery first began. In some ways it would have been easier for Jason to call in sick. He'd have no anxiety about embarrassing himself in front of smartphone-armed teenagers; he could watch as much television as he wants knowing the privacy of his bathroom is just feet away.

But the difficulty of securing a sub and writing a sub plan, of knowing his absence will cause less learning and more ambiguity and most likely veer his classes off course—it all seems like too much trouble. Even while suffering through food poisoning from a delicious seafood soup.

For Jason, like many other teachers, enduring sickness is preferable to the uncertainties of a stranger in his classroom. It's simply easier—or at least less worry. Discomfiting though it may sound, he's decided it's better to get diarrhea than a sub.

KEY IDEA

- It's often a burden to miss class because of the trouble arranging a substitute and providing instructions, and because of the decreased learning that will likely result.

Chapter 20

Phallic Gerrymandering

The lesson is going well so Phil decides to improvise. Then somehow, in one of the more embarrassing moments of his career, he inadvertently outlines a giant penis in front of his class.

They're discussing the bicameral structure of Congress and how both houses are elected. After an interesting debate about whether the Senate's two representatives from big and small states alike violates the principle of one-person-one-vote, they transition to talking about the fairness of the lower chamber. This leads naturally to eighteenth-century Massachusetts governor Elbridge Gerry, who redrew to the advantage of his own Democratic-Republican Party his home state's senate districts—one of which purported to look like a salamander. Hence gerrymandering, perhaps the most iconic portmanteau of American political discourse.

Feeling confident, Phil goes off script. He wants to bring the concept to life in a way students will never forget. Accidentally, that's exactly what he does. Around this time, Google Earth is unveiled to the public and teachers quickly see its educational potential. Phil turns on the projector and pulls down a large screen in front of the whiteboard, still facilitating the discussion. As the desktop display materializes he clicks the program's icon and a three-dimensional globe appears set against a black universe pocked with stars. A low hum of excitement fills the room.

"Check it out, guys," he begins, seemingly in control. "Let's do some gerrymandering of our own. Say you want to carve out a Republican district in a heavily Democratic area." San Francisco pops into his mind because it's both liberal and close to his school.

Phil slides his cursor to the top of the screen and selects a feature allowing him to draw connected yellow lines and therefore also rudimentary shapes. "We'll take this section here," he says, "and how about another big chunk right below it." He creates two octagonal half-circles one on top of the other like an 8 sliced vertically in half. But he wants to sketch a more intricate district so he decides to manipulate its western border. Though his back is to the students, he can feel their presence.

"Let's include another sliver right here."

From the base of the bottom half-circle he clicks once to the left and sees a long line appear down Market Street. After a final click back at the path's beginning an image appears, overlaid in bright yellow on the northeastern tip of the city. It takes him a moment to process the shape of the now-connected yellow lines, but then he sees it: two spheres and an elongated rod.

Oh please no, he says to himself, *please tell me that's NOT on the screen. Holy shit, what have you just done.* He's staring straight ahead, aware of the twenty-five teenagers looking up from behind. Phil needs to react quickly, and appropriately, or the situation could get really messy really quick. He could be out of a job.

But it's not always easy knowing how best to respond. Teenagers seem especially sensitive to double entendres and you'd be amazed how often they occur in class. In Economics, bank loans are sometimes referred to as the lube of the economy; it's nearly impossible to say "lube" in front of high schoolers and expect them to keep a straight face. Sometimes it's hard keeping a straight face yourself.

Try uttering "Woodcock Johnson," the official name of a cognitive abilities test used for placement in Special Education, in a student-support meeting with James, his mom, dad, therapist, counselor and tutor, four of your colleagues, and your assistant principal. If your lips upturn, if your eyebrows arch, if your eyes so much as squint after hearing the words Woodcock and Johnson, you will be placing yourself in an unfortunate position.[1]

There are also pitfalls in literature. On some reading lists is a novel about the Cultural Revolution in China entitled *Balzac and the Little Chinese Seamstress,* and it's often an issue. Once an English teacher tried to preempt the inevitable ribaldry by saying, "Okay everyone, get it all out." But when a student yelled, "I was so tired I fell asleep with *Balzac* on my chin last night," the teacher was unable to control himself, breaking character and cackling as hard as his students. This is one way to deal with sexual awkwardness: admit it, have a laugh, and move on.

Sometimes, however, you're unsure if the class has even taken notice. Let's say you're drawing shells and bullets on the whiteboard during a ballistics presentation, attempting to explain the meaning of "hollow-tip." The smashed slugs looked vaguely penile and you anticipate students will think the same. Not that you'd ask, of course, you just steel yourself for an inappropriate interjection.

Or maybe you're diagramming analytical body paragraphs and you shorten Argument, Evidence and Analysis to "Arg," "Evid," and "Anal." "Anal" is a funny word for teenagers, you'll learn shortly thereafter, so for the following classes you might modify the abbreviation even further to simply "An." Problem solved.

When students speak themselves they are prone to clumsy or misleading language too. During a presentation about Enlightenment philosophers, a group might write on the board Voltaire's famous yet apocryphal saying: "The Pen is Mightier than the Sword." But if some of the words smush together a few kids might start chuckling. "The Penis Mightier than the Sword."

Occasionally, innuendoes become so sexually explicit there is danger in acknowledging them at all. You can imagine what might happen during a charades review game when a student mistakes Napoleon for Neapolitan ice cream.

If you're a teacher, you've undoubtedly experienced uncomfortable moments in class, a fair number of which involve sex, and you know how imperative it is to handle them correctly. If you or a student mistakenly says or does something lewd and you think it will go unnoticed it's best not to respond; but if other students react then you're faced with a decision.

If you've drawn a variety of hollow-tip bullets on the board and they look like penises you could confess, making a joke while trying to diffuse the situation in the process. You could say, "Yes, they do look phallic . . . but let's not go ballistic." While making light of the situation is an option, you risk causing some students distress. But then again you may be perceived as less human for ignoring the gaffe altogether.

And then there's Phil, staring up at the yellow image stamped on Google Earth. His students are seniors, mostly seventeen and eighteen, some of them legal adults. Hearing laughter begin to spread throughout the room, he decides it's time to confront the consequences of his actions. He clears the screen and turns toward the class. He'll address the issue obliquely, he decides, maintaining plausible deniability.

"All right, everyone, hopefully that made an impression on you," he says with a faint grin. Then he tells students to review for several minutes in pairs and consider the positive effects of gerrymandering, which he figures will give them space to get any jokes out of their system. When they regroup many students share thoughtful responses so he decides to move on. "Well, that's our introduction to gerrymandering," he says. "I don't think any of you will soon forget it." He chuckles and adds, "I know I certainly won't."

In many ways the classroom is a microcosm of life, a reflection of humanity, a portrait of society in miniature. Along with teachers and students, innuendo occasionally slips through the door—just as double entendres punctuate the most workaday moments of one's existence.

Since teachers should avoid making inappropriate comments to students, it's imperative they handle the dirty comment, obscene illustration, or crude gesture professionally, no matter how unintentional it may be. At one point or another, every teacher will experience this dilemma. It's nearly impossible to avoid, and with any luck they'll get it right.

And hopefully, no one ever again draws a phallus over downtown San Francisco.

KEY IDEAS

- Embarrassing moments, especially of a sexual kind, sometimes arise from the performative nature of teaching.
- It is imperative to handle these moments appropriately.
- This might involve surreptitiously acknowledging the blooper, then moving on as humanly as possible.

NOTE

1. Whatever else you do, do not picture Billy Bob Thornton playing PE teacher Mr. Woodcock in the film of the same name.

Chapter 21

Let's Talk About Sex Ed

Sexual education is a necessary component of a well-rounded high-school curriculum. Hopefully middle school too. Even elementary. Regardless of the moral or ideological issues polarizing the debate, research overwhelmingly supports comprehensive sex ed in school. Among other benefits, communities with such programs have fewer unwanted pregnancies and lower rates of sexually transmitted infections among teenagers.

Though neither academics nor medical health professionals, high-school teachers have been on the frontlines of this issue for some time. And they know teaching sex ed can be challenging, slightly awkward, occasionally embarrassing, and yet almost always fun. Even when you're handling Woody the Wooden Dildo or comparing a woman's cervix to the tip of her nose.

Fortunately, many communities have wholeheartedly endorsed a comprehensive sexual education curriculum. Even so, what is actually being taught in sexual-education programs might come as some surprise to those who don't teach. It certainly has for a beginning teacher named Benjamin.

He's been gearing up for the sex ed unit over a number of weeks. Sarah, a helpful colleague, has shared with him many of her resources, including an activity called Sexual Anatomy Jeopardy. The activity includes candid questions—or answers, for the Jeopardy! purists—about foreskin, ejaculates, labia, and ovulation—like "People sometimes refer to these as women's inner and outer lips"; or, "During circumcision this is removed from the penis." One even calls for explaining the phrase "Pop your cherry" (hint: it involves the hymen).

But when Ben notices a particularly colorful question comparing an inner part of a woman's sexual reproductive system with an outer part of her face, he's momentarily taken aback. He'll have to read this question to students and they'll have to answer. Eventually the day arrives. Preparing for their sexual-anatomy quiz, the class is playing Jeopardy as review. Ben writes the five categories on the whiteboard—The Basics, All About Men, All About Ladies, We All Have One, The Menstrual Cycle—then explains the rules and gets started.

Toward the end of the last round with only a few questions and Final Jeopardy remaining, someone chooses All About Ladies for forty points. The score is close with several teams vying for first place. Scanning his clipboard, Ben discovers the question about which he has been so apprehensive.

He clears his throat. "If a woman were to reach into her vagina for this," he begins, "it would feel like the tip of her nose with a dimple in it."

He delivers the line matter-of-factly but inside feels a little uneasy. Perhaps it's the personal nature of the question, the phrasing of it. The imagery of a woman fingering her vagina seems so intimate. Maybe he should switch to the passive tense. And why, for that matter, does it have to be the hand of a woman? Guys will need to know about the answer to this question as well. By changing the wording to, "When one reaches into a vagina and touches this, it feels like the tip of his or her nose with a dimple in it," the effect might be less personal and more inclusive at the same time. Ben makes a note.

"Da-DA-da-da . . . da-DA-da," the class sings, "da-da-da-da-DA! . . . da-da-da-da-da."

The contestant huddles with her teammates.

"Okay, time's up. What's your final answer?"

"The cervix?"

"That's correct."

The girl smiles and her teammates start to cheer, clapping and patting her on the back. Evidently no one else feels weird about the question. Maybe he's just being immature, or maybe everyone's feeling a little like him on the inside.

Regardless of the subject matter kids love competitive games, Ben learns that day, and Jeopardy helps defuse the awkwardness of teenagers discussing penises and vaginas in front of their peers. It enables students to feel at ease with sensitive material. But more than anything, a comfortable teacher produces comfortable students. Kids need to be free of anxiety in order to learn so teachers must be free of anxiety while they teach. When teachers feel at peace their students will too.

When teaching sensitive material it's also important to consider the explicitness of one's language. For example, imagine you and your class are examining statistics about sexual health. One shows lesbians with lower rates of sexually transmitted infections than gay men and a student asks why. You could answer generally and say when women have sex they are less likely to transmit STIs—but that's circular reasoning and also somewhat evasive.

Or you could be blunt and explain when the penis enters the anus, which is one way gay men have intercourse, it often causes tearing, what's referred to medically as an anal fissure, and so anal sex is more likely to spread disease than oral sex or the use of a dildo, which are more common methods of lesbian intercourse. (Your noneducator friends will also enjoy this conversation so feel free to bring it up over dinner, at intramural volleyball, or with extended family.)

There's more to sex education than sexual anatomy, of course, and some teachers use The Five Circles of Sexuality as a framework. They include Sensuality (comfort and enjoyment), Intimacy (emotional attachment), Sexualization (using sex as power over others), Sexual Identity (gender roles and sexual orientation), and Sexual Health and Reproduction (sexual anatomy, birth control).

To help with these various circles, Planned Parenthood sends specialists to many schools. They do not encourage students to have sex and get abortions, nor do they rail against religious or conservative viewpoints. Students enjoy their guest speakers as a refreshing reprieve from their everyday routine. Plus, the experts keep teachers current on the latest developments in their field. Because things frequently change.

One such example, gender fluidity, is gaining greater and greater acceptance as people begin to understand the limitations of binary masculine and feminine pronouns. Some don't identify as either a man or a woman; there is much room for difference in between, and our language should reflect this diversity. Indeed, there is a growing movement to use gender neutral pronouns like "Ne," "Ve," and "Ze," or even simply "They."

Though inquiring about one's preferred pronouns has not completely permeated the mainstream, it's something sex ed teachers in particular should understand. And it illustrates why professional development for this subject is especially important.

The following week, Ben witnesses a particularly skillful Planned Parenthood health educator teach his class, and he's humbled. Sonia knows her stuff. She has already shown students the difference between the "beanie" and "sombrero" sides of a condom using Woody, a wooden penis. (Sombrero faces up, by the way.) She tells students not to stress over condoms breaking because although they are very thin they're also extremely durable.

To illustrate her point, Sonia asks for a student volunteer and an intrepid boy leaps to his feet. Telling the student to roll up his sleeve, hold out his arm, and make a fist, Sonia then stretches the condom over his hand and up to his shoulder. The class is stunned. Ben stands guard for penis jokes—"Wow, wish I was hung like that"—but hears nothing inappropriate.

In truth a little humor can be valuable but, like alcohol and inflation, too much becomes counterproductive. Especially when dealing with a delicate subject like sex ed, a relaxed classroom environment is essential. Students should feel free to share and ask questions, and inserting an occasional joke often lightens the mood, yet finding the right balance can be tricky. Fortunately, Sonia is a pro.

Next she calls up two more students for a lesson on the importance of lube. Using lube is a good way to ensure condoms don't break, she says, and also to enhance the sensation. As instructed the two boys put on latex gloves and shake hands. It's a sticky, rubbery clasp. Then Sonia squirts a dollop of K-Y Jelly in each boy's palm and they shake again, nearly slipping from each other's grip. Point taken.

By now the boys have realized their handshakes are sexual symbolism. Since Ben is supervising but not teaching directly he's taken the opportunity to talk with individual students at his desk about their semester-long research papers in order to maximize class time. From his periphery he notices the boys getting overconfident.

Just before removing their gloves they try to execute the finger-in-the-hole sex gesture. But both opt for the figurative penis—perhaps because neither wants to represent the vagina—and mid-approach touch pointer fingers instead. A metaphorical boner bump.

"Oh that's so wrong," one says.

"Eww," replies the other.

They remove their latex gloves and shake out their hands, wiping them on their jeans. Though the two boys were only messing around Ben wonders if their act should be judged offensive, and whether or not he should do something about it. Sonia is unaware and he doesn't believe many students saw either.

Ben begins to stand and address their behavior but realizes doing so will only call attention to them. Since no one appears upset, he lets it go and resumes talking with the student sitting next to him. If their prank has crossed the line he decides it isn't by much—and it hasn't adversely affected the class atmosphere.

Sonia has one more demonstration. She wants to reinforce the precept that oil-based lubricants should never be used with condoms; water-based lube only, she implores. This time Sonia dribbles baby oil on the forearm of a girl standing at the front of the room. Blowing up a condom like a balloon Sonia begins rubbing it quickly against the student's slippery limb. After a few seconds the condom pops, jolting students from their seats.

"Now you definitely don't want this to happen during sex," Sonia says, reiterating her point. "You don't want the condom to break. So what's the ONLY type of lubricant you should ever use with a condom?"

Sonia's lesson is highly engaging. Interspersed between readings and a slideshow are fun activities bolstering the main ideas she wants kids to learn.

Through her lesson planning and encouraging disposition Sonia has created an environment in which students feel comfortable talking about sex; she's equipped them with critical harm reduction strategies.

The alternative is a heavy-handed dissemination of information, a room where kids listen but do not ask questions or contribute. Worse still is the school with no sex education program at all (and abstinence-only is emphatically not sex ed).

On one hand, some argue that teaching teenagers about sex only encourages them to do more of it; that if you tell kids "Just Say No" and teach them solely about the benefits of abstinence most will refrain from intercourse until they are more mature. Unfortunately, research doesn't support this position, and it doesn't make much intuitive sense either.

As a rule it's better to give teens, like all people in general, access to as much information as possible in order to make well-informed decisions. This is true of driving, voting, drinking alcohol, using the Internet, et cetera. Young people are more likely to choose wisely amid the open marketplace of ideas.

And though this information is eminently important for young people, it can also lead to awkward and funny moments, especially for the teacher who is teaching them about sexuality. It can be challenging to instruct honestly, openly, and engagingly while making sure everyone feels at ease—especially when one is not wholly comfortable likening a woman's cervix to the tip of her nose, speaking frankly about anal fissures, or palming Woody the Wooden Dildo.

But professionalism requires nothing less. The quality of teenagers' lives, and the lives they may create somewhere down the line, will be better when pregnancy and parenthood are planned. Their lives will be fuller, richer, and more fruitful because of a first-rate sex education.

KEY IDEAS

- Sex ed is a crucial component of the high-school curriculum, and it has a demonstrably positive effect on students' lives.
- Yet teaching sex ed can also be uncomfortable for the instructor.

Chapter 22

To Be Feared or Loved

The Prince, Niccolo Machiavelli's sixteenth-century Italian treatise on political leadership, is essential reading for the modern statesmen. But it also raises compelling issues for teachers, those leaders of young men and women.

Perhaps most famously, Machiavelli questions whether it is better to be feared or loved. Though Machiavelli was examining politics, the subject is equally relevant in education. Which is more desirable for a teacher? Many rookies will notice it's easier developing a friendly rapport with students than maintaining strict authority over them. It takes too long settling down classes and too much time transitioning between activities. New teachers wear too much grief about long assignments and difficult tests.

Now imagine two classroom veterans. Spanish teacher Señor Ruiz has a shtick, the rule-oriented authoritarian. Submit to his authority and he will push you beyond your academic limits, occasionally your social limits too. His dress code rules are more severe than the school's formal policy so his students lug extra clothes solely for his class, pulling on sweatpants and sweatshirts before entering his room and removing them directly upon leaving.

If a girl's top is too low or her skirt too high, if a boy's pants hang too far below his waist, Señor will let them know. This is boot camp: dress neat, sit down, listen up—follow his rules and Señor will teach you more than you believe you're capable of learning. His methods have worked for innumerable students, opening their hearts and minds to the wonders of a beautiful yet foreign language.

Behind the scenes, Señor Ruiz drifts off in staff meetings. He sneaks a *siesta* during fire drill review or birthday announcements before rising methodically for a grand proclamation. *"Con permiso,"* he begins as if addressing a collection of international dignitaries, sermonizing about any number of questionably important topics. Among teachers, Señor is a regular person, not merely a personality. Still highly effective in the classroom—but also human. Perhaps this is the type of teacher you'd want to be.

Now picture an English teacher we'll call Mr. C. Mr. C is renowned for being able to reach even the most rambunctious of teenagers. Mr. C awards Nerd Points to students who answer challenging questions correctly. Hidden among routine queries, Nerd Questions might concern writing, literature, even current events. The student with the most points at the end of the semester will be crowned Top Nerd, receiving an automatic A regardless of his or her current grade.

What adolescents, especially those high-energy and game-oriented, do not like to compete? Plus getting a "free A" seems too good to be true. As the weeks pass, even the least engaged slip from the back of the room to the front. They realize Mr. C is more likely to call on centrally located students, which means a greater likelihood of netting points. Day after day, Mr. C dangles his bait as they read *Macbeth*, write literary analyses, and examine the difference between gerunds and participial phrases. They're hooked—and they're learning.

Think about Mr. C and Señor Ruiz and consider whom you'd like to emulate in the classroom. If you're still unsure, it may help returning to Niccolo Machiavelli. In a nod to Señor Ruiz, Machiavelli argues it's better to be feared than loved.

He writes, "[M]en love at their own free will, but fear at the will of the prince, and that a wise prince must rely on what is in his power and not on what is in the power of others." He means both fear and love are implements of authority—except a leader only has control over the former. You cannot force people to love you but you can surely make them fear you.

Though he was referring to sixteenth-century political leadership rather than twenty-first-century teaching, the tension is nonetheless apropos. In the classroom, who do you want to be? Are you the funny man or the taskmaster, the comedian or the drill sergeant? And which identity creates the most suitable environment for learning?

If Machiavelli were a professor of education he may have asked whether it's better to be liked or respected. One clue lies in the pedagogue's attire. Younger teachers often dress more formally to gain respect but as their careers progress they shed the sartorial splendor in favor of something more comfortable.

As teachers grow old, legitimacy and respect come somewhat easier so one's uniform matters less and less, though it's harder and harder to stay relevant, relate to teenagers, and thus remain well liked. Both deference and uncoolness, it seems, are natural by-products of aging. You no longer need to convince anyone of your authority—only that you're still relevant.

In reality, adoration and reverence are equally desirable characteristics and choosing between them is a false dilemma. The question is one of degree. Some teachers are loved by students, they enjoy a cult of personality and are consistently fun but they're also perceived as easy and thus lack respect and often the ability to control. When teachers entertain yet don't require much of students it's easy to be well liked. But this doesn't always translate into respect, nor does it equate to learning.

Sometimes it's necessary for students to grind, to get dirty in the intellectual trenches, and in these moments, respect is key. Some teachers are great at dominating a room and commanding silence. They compel students to work but the result is often learning that is coerced and therefore inferior. Emphasizing respect at the expense of affection can be equally unhelpful. The best-case scenario is a hybrid of the two, part Señor Ruiz, part Mr. C.

In a perfect world, teachers would be equally liked and respected. They would be loved like a relative—but also feared the way a son knows never to cross his father. If students learn from Señor Ruiz because they have to, they learn from Mr. C because he lets them enjoy it. In truth, both love and fear are necessary instruments of effective teaching. The real mystery lies in determining the balance.

So as Machiavelli the education professor might say to his princely pupils, "Students like at their own free will, but respect at the will of the teacher, and the wise teacher must do what is in his or her power to achieve both."

KEY IDEAS

- It can be tempting for teachers to create a persona emphasizing either fear or love in the classroom.
- But ideally, teachers will be at once well liked and well respected by their students.

Chapter 23

Roll Tape

Among teachers there's a common phrase about giving minimum effort in the classroom. Similar to a postman "mailing it in," the expression conjures images of a special form of slouch: the physical educator. No, not "Those who can't do, teach. And those who can't teach, teach gym"—that would contravene most teachers' beliefs and experience. But nonetheless it's a humorous line.

When teachers choose to give less than their best, to take a period off or even lose hope in their careers entirely, they often say it's time to "roll out the balls." Picture the hirsute, short-shorted PE teacher seated in the bleachers with a clipboard and whistle reading the morning's newspaper. He empties a rack of basketballs, volleyballs, and dodgeballs and students do whatever they please, which usually means nothing at all.

The classroom equivalent to rolling out the balls—you may have guessed—is showing a movie. In a nod to the phrase's athletic progenitor, it's also called "rolling tape." Sometimes the popular perception of teachers in general suggests their job is quite easy. They have two months of summer as well as several weeks around the holidays and scattered throughout the year, and when not vacationing they're presumably not working very hard either, particularly if they're not the Sage on the Stage.

In social studies classes in particular, teachers show numerous films. Documentaries, independents, Hollywood epics, even the occasional made-for-TV special. Though sometimes these teachers may feel guilty about rolling tape, behind the scenes, and the screen, lies an important question: What role should movies play in the classroom? The lead, a bit part, or a cameo? What impact do they have on student learning?

At their best, movies bring content to life, animating a subject the way little else can. In World History, for example, many teachers show the History

Channel's French Revolution documentary. Some break it into segments aligning with particular phases of the revolution: beginning with the Enlightenment through the Great Fear, continuing with King Louis's trial through the Reign of Terror, and culminating several days later with Napoleon's coronation and the end of the film. Other teachers show the whole documentary at once as reinforcement after having studied the revolution in its entirety.

Either way, if students are reading, writing, and speaking about a pivotal moment in history, it makes sense for them to *see* it as well. Plus, if a picture is worth a thousand words then a movie, a motion picture, is surely worth at least a million. If you envision the academic substance of your own high-school career, be it Shakespeare, the Cold War, or plate tectonics, many of those images are undoubtedly derived from film.

Watching movies in class also likely represented for you a singular moment of joy. One can still hear the squeaking wheels of the obsidian double-decker audiovisual cart rolling down the halls, still see the thirty-two-inch cathode ray tube television strapped to the cart's upper level like cargo on the roof of a minivan, or still remember the even greater thrill of being summoned to retrieve the cart from the AV room oneself.

And when as a teacher, after telling students they'll be watching a movie, one sees broad smiles and the intermittent fist pump, one can recall with heartening empathy the happiness that is generated by rolling tape. Kids love it, and it helps them learn.

As awesome as Movie Day is for students, it's only effective if they're paying attention. Sometimes teenagers conflate the excitement of watching films with permission to drift off, believing entertainment and distraction are analogous. *I can just relax and zone out*, they might think, which is one reason teachers create movie guides. They want students to enjoy the experience but they also want them engaged, internalizing key points, and a handout with a list of questions is a good way to ensure students are focused.

Yet while having kids listen for predetermined questions might force them to follow along more closely, scribbling answers as they look up from their papers and down from the screen, it can also kill the thrill—and cause a distracting myopia. For example, if you're waiting intently on the name of the publisher of the radical French Revolution newspaper *L'Ami du peuple*, you may fail to appreciate other details as they pass by, like so many unseen vistas down a highway. If you're frantically searching for answers you may not see the forest for the trees.

For these reasons it may be preferable to cut a deal with students. There will be no movie guides to fill out, you promise them, as long as you receive something in return. "If I give you the blessing of watching this movie without writing anything down," you say, "you guys must give me your full, undivided attention, and nothing less. You can pack up everything," you tell them, "except for your focus and your enthusiasm for World History—keep those right in front of you."

When it's going well, Movie Day is great for teachers and students alike. Kids relish the opportunity to "do nothing," while teachers merely press Play, adjust the volume, then retreat to the soft glow of the computer screen behind their desk. It can seem so easy it's like you're not really teaching at all (though much work is secretly involved in creating an attentive environment).

But how tired one is at the end of the day, how much one's throat hurts or patience is tested is not the metric by which a given practice should be evaluated. The essential question is: will a particular instructional strategy help kids learn more than another? It's not: how hard does it feel like I'm working?

Of course, too much of a good thing can be bad. What was once a special occasion, a treat, may turn gluttonous. When watching movies becomes commonplace, students will find them less compelling, which means they'll be less engrossed and therefore learn less as well. But an appropriately timed film, toward the end of a unit of study, say every four to six weeks, can truly bring a concept to life.

And as much as students benefit from the images, dialogue, and music giving texture to the words they've previously read, it's the debrief process that's perhaps most impactful. Students themselves talking about what they learned, questions that emerged, the ideas with which they agreed and disagreed.

In essence, a movie is an input method. Sights and sounds. One can also learn from written words (a book), or sounds alone (a lecture), but one way or another information must reach the brain through one's eyes and ears. It's what happens afterward, what students do with these inputs, that truly matters.

Movies don't have to be movies either. The Internet allows teachers to show short clips effortlessly—as a hook to get students' attention, a transition between activities, a discussion starter, or a review. Brief videos can break up large blocks of time and serve a number of different purposes.

Like human beings, videos come in all forms and sizes. Some are longer and shorter, some enchanting, and others quite dull. Some are tolerable in quick spurts while others take time to fully comprehend. At their best, movies can animate abstract concepts and previous chapters of civilization. And as an instructional reprieve they can reach the pinnacle of classroom enjoyment for both students and teachers. Except really it's no reprieve at all—just a different strategy, another method of teaching and learning. When used effectively and in moderation, watching films can feel deeply gratifying, a signal pleasure.

Though it might seem like rolling out the balls, like you've given up or thrown in the towel, rolling tape is an effective practice, an oft-maligned yet sound teaching technique. It can do for students what the silver screen has always aspired to do for its audiences: education through entertainment.

KEY IDEA

- Showing movies in class is valuable, not only because everyone enjoys them but also because movies effectively augment student learning.

Section IV

IN LOCO PARENTIS

Chapter 24

B2SN

The parents have arrived. Some are wandering like puzzled freshmen with faces buried in schedules and maps, stumbling through the courtyard and into the building while others, having attended innumerable Back to School Nights, zip past with purpose, navigating campus deftly.

"Excuse me, where's room 904?" a friendly couple asks. Casey is lingering on the periphery, still hesitant to enter his room.

"Two classes over," he says and reluctantly points to Raul's open door. These are the Early Birds, the ones who either don't know about the principal's introductory speech in the main gym or who have consciously chosen to ignore it.

Standing in the hallway, Casey is trying to avoid the fate of Raul, who will soon be corralled by inquisitive parents until the official commencement of teacher presentations. So Casey wanders the halls and into other rooms, blending with the Early Birds like an intelligence operative, a textbook evasion maneuver.

At the last minute, Casey returns from his clandestine walkabout to a full classroom. Though he tells himself to relax and have fun, that it doesn't really matter, he knows this is an important moment. Along with Open House in the spring, this is one of two evenings all year when parents enter classrooms. But Back to School Night, known in Teacherland as B2SN, is arguably more significant since it's the first impression.

The stakes are high because you want parents to like you and trust you and respect you, to believe their children are in capable hands. You want parents feeling comfortable for their own peace of mind but also so they'll grant you the necessary latitude to teach—and support you if issues with their son or daughter happen to arise.

If parents begin questioning your practice the school year can become a lengthy slog; but if they believe you're a skillful educator it will proceed quickly, smoothly. And they'll form their opinions of you based in large part on your ten-minute talk one night in September. So you need to have a plan, and you need to execute.

With less than a minute before the bell rings, Casey tells parents to grab a note card and writing utensil if they've not already done so from the desk near the front of the room. In addition to Casey's name and contact info on the whiteboard—and a large "Thank you, Parent Foundation!"—he also includes directions for a task. He asks parents to write their names, their student's name, their contact info, and one thing Casey should know about their sons and daughters that might help Casey teach them a little better.

There are two reasons for this initial activity, one sneaky and the other sincere. The first is a filibuster: if parents are busy writing there will be less room for potentially compromising small talk. The second is a rare opportunity for insight: from the note cards Casey is able to glean useful information about students he's still getting to know, like who is deathly shy and hates being called on, who is an aspiring ballet dancer and maintains a demanding schedule, and who just moved from Ventura Beach because his mom recently divorced his dad and his friends are still there but he's hoping to start school on the right foot.

As the bell rings Casey takes a deep breath and dives in. He's aiming for maximum energy, passion, and excitement, even levity too. He hears several reassuring chuckles and presses on, saying he's going to talk a little about himself and then the class. Which, if you were a parent, is what you'd probably want to know. Who is this person standing in front of you? Do they seem knowledgeable about their subject? Are they caring and fair and kind?

Casey begins by discussing his youthful adventures in the music business then transitions into the details of geometry. In subsequent years he'll feel increasingly uncomfortable talking about himself and instead proceed directly into the curriculum but for now he's trying to use his background to gain points and hopefully earn some credibility, which he may be subconsciously insecure about lacking.

Midway through an overview of the course content he hears a phone ring. He's standing down the middle aisle near the back wall between rows of parents seated facing each other like guests across a long dinner table. Spinning around to quip that he's going to confiscate the device as he would a student's he sees—to his dismay—a father hunched over his desk with a hand pressed to his left ear and a phone stuck furtively against his right. The father is a prominent businessman, Casey learns later, and his wife a journalist for the local paper.

"Hello?" the father whispers. "Hey. Yes, we can reschedule it for tomorrow."

Casey sees other parents with fraught faces glaring at the father on his phone. "Wow," Casey mouths quietly and registers a few affirming gestures in response. It seems many of these parents are like their kids: most are engaged with inviting expressions, others are struggling to appear attentive, and a few have lost focus entirely (not to mention the one currently taking a phone call).

Perhaps this is a reflection of the many behaviors students exhibit in class, a manifestation of some greater biological experiment at play. Or maybe these parents represent the human condition as a whole—how any group of people will act while listening passively. The same is true of teachers themselves, after all, at staff meetings.

The power-broking father solidifies his morning schedule. "Okay, I gotta go," he says and slips his phone into his jacket. At this point Casey is considering saying something to the oblivious father but instead he pushes forward, knowing there are only a few minutes left. Casey is nearly finished when the bell rings so he wraps up. "Well, looks like that's it. Sorry we don't have more time. It's been really nice talking with you. Remember to leave the info cards on your desks. Have a nice night!"

Actually the bell is an interruption for which Casey has been planning, a thinly veiled ploy. He's trying to avoid filling dead airtime with parent questions. While most will be good-natured, they can also lead to unnecessarily unpleasant exchanges, usually involving grading and homework. So he gabs until the bell rings and feigns ignorance—"Whoops, time to go!"—then stands by the door and ushers everyone out with a smile.

Upon leaving, many parents pause to introduce themselves and say hello. If you were in their position you'd likely do the same, and as a teacher it's nice connecting moms and dads to the students with whom you've been building relationships for the first several weeks of school. Since everyone must hurry to the next class presentation, though, there's only time for a brief handshake and greeting.

Soon the line dissipates and a new group funnels in.

"Be sure to grab an index card from the front of the room and fill it out," Casey says, beginning the exhibition anew. After four more ten-minute presentations split up by two short reprieves—since Casey teaches five of seven periods—the affair appears to be over. An administrator announces over the intercom that Back to School Night is finished, thanking parents for coming and wishing them a wonderful evening as his colleagues do a perimeter sweep to clear the area.

At this point many teachers dash for their automobiles. Not only are they ready to leave after a twelve-hour day but they also fear getting trapped by The Straggler. The Straggler is the last parent who, unintentionally or not, waits until everyone has left in order to entertain a private conversation. Some teachers are eminently accommodating, talking late after the final bell until The Straggler has been sated. Other teachers will abscond with jackets half on and bags in the crook of an elbow, leery of parents following closely behind. It is said a few Stragglers have even followed teachers to their cars.

If Casey can escape safely he faces one final decision: have a nightcap or head home. He's pulsing with energy, fueled by the significance of his performance, and it can be difficult falling asleep. Plus it's fun to share highlights with colleagues—like the parent who just took a phone call in class.

On this night, even though he's planning to rise early the next morning for a run, he decides to meet some coworkers for a drink. Casey and his friends sit alongside the bar, talking about embarrassing slip-ups and impolitic parents. In this moment they feel like a team, a fraternity, members of a secret club who perform bizarre rituals unfamiliar to the outside world.

As Casey is about to leave he receives a message from another teacher friend. It's a picture of Casey mid-routine, leaning against a bookcase with his legs crossed, gesticulating spiritedly in a blur of movement, apparently taken from the low angle of a desk. Studying the image, he realizes it's been tagged and posted on several social networks by a parent. The caption is flattering but he's taken aback nonetheless, somewhat uncomfortable with the now-public nature of this once-private event. Perhaps he should've known parents would be social networking in class—after all they're more like their children than they might imagine.

On the drive home, having begun to wind down, Casey recalls the evening that's just passed in a flurry of speeches and handshakes and smiles. He hopes parents on this annual night back to school feel comfortable with their children's math teacher and with his curriculum. He hopes they think he's a caring person and able professional, and he hopes this means they'll support him with a wide berth, adequate discretion, and sufficient latitude to instruct.

He hopes he has put on a good show.

KEY IDEAS

- Back to School Night is a momentous event, as parents make first impressions and form opinions about the caretakers of their offspring.
- Teachers' goal for Back to School Night is to ensure parents feel comfortable about their abilities and with who they are as people, which includes the added benefit of less parental oversight throughout the year.

Chapter 25

Parental Cocktail Party

"Danni, guess we better put some stuff on the walls."

Danni's teaching partner Paul, who has just walked into her room, is rolling out a yearly inside joke. They bat it around.

"But they're already filled with posters and projects."

"Those are old. How are we going to show parents what students have learned *this* year?

It's the morning of Open House and their conversation masks a genuine desire to formulate a plan for the evening.

"Hey," Paul says, shifting tone, since both share students in an English–social studies teaching collaborative, "we could combine classes and be in the same room, take a little pressure off."

The school day passes and soon Paul is back in Danni's classroom, neither of them having figured out what they're going to do. They procrastinate further with a quick workout and a burrito. When they return, freshen up and change clothes, about an hour remains before parents will begin to arrive. They decide to stay in their own rooms, each eventually flopping an assortment of books and papers on desks near the door.

Feeling a pang of insecurity, Danni at the last minute grabs several laptops and displays various student projects for parents to peruse while waiting their turn to talk with her. She also projects her website on a pull-down screen against the front wall (in past years she'd create a rolling slideshow of students in action, laughing, collaborating, learning their hearts out, which was always entertaining but became, she decided at some point, not worth the effort of production).

Unlike the ritualized dog-and-pony show of Back to School Night in which teachers address a room of captive parents, Open House is something of a pedagogical cocktail party—a parent–teacher networking event. Relaxed and informal, held in the spring instead of the fall, Open House functions like its real estate namesake. Teachers open their doors and parents walk through inspecting the scholastic layout, the curricular furnishings, the educational decor.

Whereas on Back to School Night parents shuffle from one presentation to another, retracing their children's footsteps like pilgrims along the Camino de Santiago, at Open House they wander from room to room at their leisure, popping in, popping out, staying for indeterminate periods of time.

In elementary and middle school and even high school, for subjects like the sciences and fine arts, much physical work is produced that can be showcased to parents. And there's a clear benefit in examining the classroom itself for evidence of learning, as one would inspect a potential home for signs of disrepair.

But the stated goal of Open House is somewhat at odds with reality. Parents want to see how their children are doing, to learn about their development, yet the evening's official purpose is to meet teachers and examine curriculum. Discussing student progress is expressly prohibited—at least in theory. Indeed, a structural defect exists in the foundation of Open House: there's not enough room for conversations with parents. Some banter and a little interaction, sure, but nothing of substance.

Let's imagine the first couple of the evening has just walked through your classroom door. "Hi, I'm Mary Littleton and this is my husband Gus," the mother says.

"Oh, nice to meet you!" you respond, racing to summon their daughter's name—if they don't happen to mention it—and an image of her face. "Nicole is great. She's super sweet and really smart too."

Now if this happens to be true, the dialogue should be easy and enjoyable. But if Nicole is a student in need of genuine guidance, because she's insufficiently engaged or missing assignments or struggling with literacy, you will need to have a candid conversation with her parents. Which can be difficult while pairs of similarly devoted parents, who seem to have mysteriously arrived, stare at you simultaneously.

You might try a compliment sandwich: "Nicole is really sweet and I'm really enjoying having her in class. It would be great, though, if she completed homework more consistently." You lean in a little closer. "I actually think she may need some extra reading support. But she works hard and I know she's going to get it."

After listening to your feedback, Nicole's parents will want to talk further, to understand what you see as their daughter's weaknesses. This is where things get tricky. You could go into detail about fluency and decoding and the Lexile scale but you risk alienating other parents, who may get fed up and leave, for the sake of appeasing Nicole's. On the other hand, if you don't follow up with Mary and Gus you risk annoying them too since you've just opened the door to a larger conversation about their daughter's performance, which you're now trying to shut.

In a best-case scenario you spend two to three minutes with each set of parents. You offer specific praise of their teenager, a nicety showing you know her well, slip in a growth area if needed, return to more praise, and conclude with an offer to schedule a meeting if they would like to talk further. Expressing their gratitude parents will then follow with a few commendations of their own—what their daughter says about you at home—and if you're lucky they may even label you her "favorite teacher." Everyone shakes hands and smiles as the next couple steps forward.

On good nights a steady trickle of parents enter your classroom. Not so few that conversations last tens of minutes but also not so many that there's a lengthy backlog of couples waiting for their chance to talk, looking at their watches, ensuring their collective body language is shouting, "Hurry up already!" In which case you may feel like installing ticket machines à la the butcher or deli counter.

Fortunately, most will arrive cheerful. Parents tend to visit teachers whom their kids most admire and it's usually a lovefest all around. "Mom, you have to see my physics teacher. She's my favorite!" And whereas few students attend the formalized proceedings of Back to School Night, many more come to Open House, knowing teachers are apt to shower them with praise—best of all in front of their parents. In truth, Open House can be a joy. It's great talking with adults who are themselves cool people about their sons and daughters for whom you genuinely care.

As with all conversation, there can be awkward moments, of course, but they're essential to the beauty of social interaction. There is much pleasure and excitement to be found in the offhand quip filling a vacant pause, the rhythms of a graceful exchange, the inherent honesty in improvisation. Yet even the liveliest dialogue with parents can sour.

This night Paul is approached toward the end of the evening by a mom and her son. Wearing high heels and a business suit, the mom speaks with her arm draped over her son's shoulder. She's very friendly. Several times during their conversation, however, Paul notices her eyes drift down to his shoes and up again; he hears what should be chuckles become full-throated guffaws. "Call me anytime," she mentions on more than one occasion.

True, Paul could be misreading the situation, but her son's expression, prostrate and suppressing a grimace, seems to corroborate his intuition. Then, as she's walking away, her son several steps ahead, the mom clutches the meat of Paul's triceps, squeezes gently, and slides her hand down his arm to his wrist. "Call anytime," she repeats, looking at him squarely as she walks out the door, her eyes lingering over her twisted neck.

For Danni, in a room with papers and books scattered across the desks, laptops exhibiting student projects and a website projected against the front wall, there are no flirtatious encounters. The parental cocktail party unravels platonically and soon the throng of guests has subsided. When the room empties she walks down the hall to see Paul. He's finishing up with two parents, nodding and laughing at all the right moments, interjecting thoughtful snippets when appropriate. "All right, okay, good night," he says as the final couple exits his room.

He turns to Danni. "Dude."

And in that word Paul transforms from a teacher to Danni's friend, as if the camera's red light has just shut off and he's no longer an on-air television personality.

"I don't think we needed to put out any papers tonight," Danni says.

"I know. No one ever looks at them."

"But, hey, at least we had plenty of stuff on the walls."

They should leave right away but Paul can't resist telling Danni about his inappropriate encounter. Eventually they turn to the value of the evening itself.

Open House may well call for elimination or replacement with parent–teacher conferences. The necessarily frank conversations needed with certain parents are impossible to accomplish in several minutes behind a crowd of onlookers, yet it seems there are some good outcomes nonetheless. Parents hear many positive words about their children, many of which aren't exaggerated, and this makes the parents, in turn, feel good too.

Teachers serve a community and it's important that community believes they're doing a good job. It's also nice when teachers hear compliments from students via their parents. Though Open House can seem like 120 minutes of small talk, like a professional mixer, it can also feel deeply reaffirming. But the structure does suffer a key flaw: parents are barred from talking about their children's progress—which is exactly what they want to do, and it most certainly happens anyway. In the end, like so much else in life, Open House's utility may diverge from its intended purpose.

Paul and Danni are getting in too deep when another teacher, their friend Pat, enters the room with a backpack over one shoulder and an empty lunch bag in his hand. "What are you guys still doing here?" he exclaims. "It's time to go!"

"Yeah, the cocktail party is over," says Danni.

"You're right," Paul adds, "I just wish we could serve drinks."

KEY IDEAS

- Open House feels like a networking event or a professional mixer.
- Though it's nice sharing commendations with parents, the environment is insufficient for providing meaningful student feedback.

Chapter 26

Parents Just Don't Understand

In 1989, before both the Internet and social media, kids watched MTV to learn about new music. One particular record in a burgeoning genre some still refused to legitimate was especially intoxicating. Written by DJ Jazzy Jeff and Will Smith, known then as The Fresh Prince, "Parents Just Don't Understand" won the first-ever Grammy for Best Rap Performance, signaling the song's allure and hip-hop's ultimate ascendancy.

Whether or not they knew it at the time, DJ Jazzy Jeff and The Fresh Prince had etched a phrase onto the bathroom walls of the American lexicon. Though many kids coming of age in the 1980s and 1990s may have been too young to entirely relate, the sentiment resonates nonetheless: how could parents ever understand what it's like to be a kid?

Asking two variations of the question, dual riffs on that moving tune, is instructive. First, how can parents understand what it's like to be a student, what their kids are doing in school? Parents may call upon their own decade and a half of desk-sitting experience—"Back in my day, son"—as a point of reference. They may talk with their children about what has recently transpired in class, examine the readings, activities, tests, and projects students bring home, and review the various resources teachers publish online.

Parents may also attend school functions to visit classrooms and meet teachers. From all this evidence, some direct, some circumstantial, they should be able to reach reasonable conclusions about the character of their kids' education.

Given the growing ubiquity of video cameras in modern life, incidentally, one might wonder how long it will be before parents demand the right to surveil their children in class. On the bodies of police officers, at doggy day care, above the nests of bald eagles, and in the hands of most students, cameras are transforming society's understanding of and desire for transparency.

For example, teachers are now expected to maintain an active website and online gradebook. It's not difficult to envision the day in which live, password-protected classroom feeds become the norm.

While the urge to monitor one's children is certainly understandable, it's fairly difficult to accomplish when they're at school. So districts assume certain responsibilities under the legal doctrine *in loco parentis* (Latin for "in the place of a parent"). And since teachers are in some capacity acting as moms and dads, it's important to understand what they do and how, not merely appreciate the fruits of their production. Not only the juice but also the squeeze.

Thus the second question: how can parents understand what it's like to teach? This is trickier than the first. Whereas it's fairly possible to determine what students are doing in class absent direct observation, it's nearly impossible to infer anything meaningful about the perspective of the teacher. Parents might assume they know what it's like to teach because they were once students and now attend yearly Back to School Nights and Open Houses as adults.

Many teachers don't give the subject much consideration either; without kids themselves they never really have to. But if and when teachers do become parents, they'll be in a better position to understand the educational issues their sons and daughters will face—issues that should be important to all parents concerned about the quality of their children's education. To consider what it means to be a student but not a teacher, then, is to miss an essential part of the story.

In a strange way, one can learn about the lives of teachers by contemplating the life of a cook. In *Kitchen Confidential* Anthony Bourdain writes, "If the chef is anything like me, the cooks are a dysfunctional, mercenary lot, fringe-dwellers motivated by money, the peculiar lifestyle of cooking and a grim pride." He says being a cook requires endurance and character and punctuality, speed and memory and toughness.

Reading *Kitchen Confidential*, you begin to understand life in the kitchen is a frenzied and often masochistic symphony that somehow, some way, turns out consistent and delicious food. And that chefs' personal lives often mirror this dynamic. Bourdain forces you to regard chefs differently—to think about them at all. If you haven't read *Kitchen Confidential* you might assume you know what it's like to cook because you've sat at various restaurant tables eating meals mysteriously prepared by a culinary stranger. You might infer from the food what it's like in the kitchen.

The restaurant industry's desire to propagate the image of discerning professionals, white-puffy-hatted, working elegantly, ethically, behind the swinging doors of the kitchen, is understandable. This illusion makes dining more pleasurable if also more fictitious. And it keeps customers happy.

But if you knew what really occurs in the kitchen, how such wonderful fare is turned out with precision at breakneck speed, if you realized who was preparing your food, and why, you'd be more appreciative of the experience—and also in a better position to make informed gastronomical decisions. Like abstaining from the Sunday tuna nicoise or Monday seafood buffet, as Bourdain infamously discloses.

You'd also realize your choices about what, where, and how to eat affect not only your palate but also the country. You may know upon reflection your plate of pasta puttanesca reveals little about the men and women who prepared it; you just probably haven't thought much about them.

In that light, *Teacherland* aspires to be the *Kitchen Confidential* of education. *Classroom Confidential* as it were. So in the spirit of Anthony Bourdain: if your child's teachers are anything close to the norm, they are rule-followers, pleasers, and lovers of learning, motivated both by a desire to do good and live well. Being a teacher takes patience and dexterity and empathy, curiosity and humor and control. Life in the classroom is a lively and often humbling performance that somehow, some way, turns out consistently well-educated young men and women.

So how can parents, or anyone, for that matter, understand what it's like to teach? What it's like to be a teacher? Other than reading about it, of course, you can stop by a teacher's classroom anytime (after getting a pass from the front office). Their doors are always open. Come see what they're cooking.

KEY IDEA

- If parents had a better understanding of what it's truly like to teach, their students would be more successful in particular, and national education policy would be more effective in general.

Section V

STUDENT, SCHOLAR, TEENAGER, KID

Chapter 27

When You Least Expect It

Ashley walks into Bing's classroom one day in the spring semester of her senior year and hands him an envelope. Then she turns to leave.

Initially Bing thinks the delivery is intended for a student but he's on a prep period and his class is empty. Puzzled, he flips it over and notices his last name written on the front cover. At once both intrigued and apprehensive he pauses momentarily before opening the flap. Ever since a fateful conversation one afternoon during her freshman year, the relationship between Ashley and Bing has been strained. Bing taught Ashley once more as a sophomore but never again after that.

In this particular conversation during Ashley's freshman year, Bing shared with her an observation, tried to offer some insight and guidance about the direction of her life as he saw it, but she seemed to react poorly, or a least awkwardly, and he never knew how she felt about the interaction. Until today.

From time to time over the next few years Bing would read about Ashley in the school newspaper or see her likeness on a promotional drama poster. She appeared to be doing well but the evidence he gathered was piecemeal and in passing. When Ashley and Bing crossed paths on campus they usually made eye contact and said hello though more often than not the exchanges felt forced.

Clearly much lay beneath the surface. Bing had tried once to access it, to help in some small way, but the conversation had changed things between them. Passing in the halls was no longer the breezy give-and-take as with most students. An unspoken weight hung over their interactions, however brief and sporadic they may have been.

Now and then Bing had wanted to check in with Ashley to find out how she was doing, ask if everything was okay, see if they needed to talk again. He considered approaching her counselor, with whom he had a good relationship and who would surely provide sound advice. Her counselor might even call Ashley in for a talk of their own. Bing oscillated between wanting to ask Ashley if what he said had made her feel uncomfortable and knowing that, whatever her reaction, she had needed to hear it. Each time he came down on the side of the latter.

What Bing said was right and appropriate, he decided, and better to hear it from a teacher during her freshman year than someone else down the road, better than no one at all. Several years later may have been too late: one makes so many choices big and small over the course of a high-school career that it can be difficult to see the starting block when the finish line is in sight. After so many twists and turns you get pointed in a certain direction, unable to retrace the arc of your life.

Staring down at the back of the envelope, Bing thumbs a diagonal seam, ripping a small aperture in the flap. Snatching a mechanical pencil lying on his keyboard, he runs it along the top crease, which at first rumples then splits cleanly down the line. A single sheet of lined paper lies folded into thirds and tucked neatly inside. Through its diaphanous exterior Bing spots rounded lettering handwritten in black ink.

He removes the paper, sets the envelope aside, and begins to read.

As my time in high school comes to an end I am starting to think about how each teacher has affected me. When I think about my experience in your class I think of a certain conversation I had with you, one that I doubt you even remember. In my freshman year you emailed my science teacher asking her to tell me to go see you after school. Naturally, I was terrified . . . was I in trouble? When I went to your classroom, you began the conversation by telling me that I was a great student and that I could have many great opportunities if I applied myself and made the right decisions.

You then said that you didn't think that my group of friends at the time were the right people for me to associate with. My immediate reaction was to get defensive and to disagree, but in my heart I knew you were right. I had felt the same way for a while but I needed someone to tell me for me to truly acknowledge that I needed to make a change. The following year, I broke away from those people and that was the best decision I ever made.

If I had stayed with that group, I would not have done many of the things that have made me who I am; and I thank you for that. I know it isn't really necessary to write this to you but I felt that you deserve my appreciation because of how much I have benefited from that conversation. So, thank you for prompting me to make a crucial decision and also for everything you taught me.

—Ashley

Bing drops the letter and stares across the empty room, exultant. This is not the sort of note he's expecting, least of all from her. Ashley's even countenance over the past four years, including minutes earlier handing him the envelope, offered no hint of her true feelings. Bing is feinted, sucker-punched with joy.

Not often did Bing receive heartfelt praise like this from students. Even the ones with whom he'd built strong relationships and for whom he'd developed an affinity, those most likely to visit as upperclassmen and while home from college, even then he might be greeted with "your class was fun," or occasionally, "your class was my favorite," but rarely anything more effusive than that. Rarely did he hear directly from current or former students about his impact.

Bing plucks Ashley's letter from his desk and reads it again. *When I think about my experience in your class I think of a certain conversation I had with you, one that I doubt you even remember.* How could he forget? It had sharply altered the nature of their interactions ever since, resurfacing in his mind regularly upon seeing her.

He pauses at the valediction: *So, thank you for prompting me to make a crucial decision and also for everything you taught me.* It seems like what Ashley learned in math was almost an afterthought, as if she were obliged to mention the actual substance of class.

It's as telling for what Ashley says as for what she doesn't. While teachers devote the bulk of their professional attention to curriculum, it may not be the most important thing they impart. Curriculum is but a planet in the infinite universe of student interaction. Teachers tend to think everything revolves around the content they so desperately want students to learn, but at the core of a high-school experience lies something infinitely more animating.

Like the famous quote apocryphally attributed to John Lennon that "life is what happens while you're busy making other plans," learning is what happens while teachers are preoccupied trying to teach. They spend so much time polishing the perfect lesson, refining the outcomes of a unit, crafting the trajectory of a class that it can be easy to forget they're teaching *people.* Teenagers who'll spend more time with them than their parents; adolescents who, whether they know it or not, crave guidance simply by virtue of being young.

When people in education talk about teaching "the whole child," this is what they mean. They mean school is more than merely the sum of classes and grades; it's everything that happens in and around and between. In school, kids learn how to exist in the presence of others, how to be part of a community; they make decisions about who they want to become and in what type of society they want to live, and in these situations teachers have a role to play.

Bing didn't have to approach Ashley—surely he had plenty of planning to do, emails to answer, grading to finish—and some might say he should not have talked to her at all, that it wasn't his place; they might say notify her counselor instead. But relegating educators to a narrow focus on curriculum misses an important opportunity to teach.

Eyeing Ashley's letter, Bing is struck by another comment, the penultimate sentence he's nearly overlooked, tucked behind her heartening send-off. *I know it isn't really necessary to write this to you but I felt that you deserve my appreciation because of how much I have benefited from that conversation.* She's right: it's not necessary. And to Bing it makes all the difference in the world.

Ashley didn't have to write Bing a letter but he'd tell you how grateful he is that she did. Ashley should remind all teachers there is more to a class than its content, more to learning than letters on a report card. She shows how you never know which kids you'll reach, nor when. Sometimes you can go weeks, months, even years unaware of your influence.

And sometimes, when you least expect it, a student will remind you just how wholly life-affirming teaching can feel.

KEY IDEAS

- Teachers teach students, rather than simply their curriculum.
- Keeping this in mind can lead to profound and meaningful interactions with young people.

Chapter 28

She Looks Like a Referee

It's toward the end of morning break and students are milling about Rob's classroom. When Jenna walks in, Rob immediately notices her outfit. Wearing a blouse with thick, vertical, black-and-white stripes and a sporty black collar, she looks rather unfortunately like a referee.

He wonders if her jersey has a square block R on the back like an official from the National Football League and the jokes hit him like a linebacker, swallowing him in a dog pile of sarcasm. He desperately wants to throw an imaginary yellow flag, blow his finger-made whistle, put both hands on his hips and yell, "Offside. Number fifty-three defense. Repeat third down."

"Hey, Jenna, good morning," he says instead, summoning every ounce of maturity not to ask if she's leaving after class to work a game, who's playing, and if she admires the work of Ed Hochuli. Jenna is a quiet young woman struggling with self-confidence and her parents' recent divorce and though Rob hopes she'll come out of her shell, he fears such needling will backfire. So he lets it slide. As class ends he avoids the urge to wish her good luck and have a nice game. Instead, Rob walks across the hall where his teacher friends are gathering for lunch.

"Did you see Jenna's shirt today?" he asks his teaching partner.

"Nope."

"But you had her first period."

"I did, why?"

"That black-and-white top? Come on, she looked like a referee. It was amazing—I almost said something."

The comment sparks a lunchroom conversation they haven't rehashed in some time. Rob and his colleagues begin recounting familiar tales of teenage farce and the equally farcical responses they engender from teachers.

"Shut the door," someone advises.

Rob's friend, William, opens with an account of a tall, awkward young man named Skip. While intelligent, Skip is also excessively formal, direct, straightforward. One day Skip comes rushing into William's class very concerned because he needs to print out his homework but the hard disk he's holding requires a Mac instead of a PC.

Since at this time their school was PC-only, William directs Skip to his colleague, Keith, who happens to have the only Mac lab on campus. Except William neglects to inform Keith of his approaching visitor, and when Skip arrives he and Keith have a bit of a miscommunication. Eventually Skip leaves, homework still trapped on his hard disk.

William, like an improv actor breaking character, can barely recite the story without giggling. At which point everyone looks at Molly. Molly has another well-worn anecdote about this same young man everyone wants retold. She's initially hesitant but relents.

A number of years ago, she says, Molly had Skip as a freshman for sex ed. During a sexual anatomy lesson in which the labia minora, majora, urethra, and vagina are identified, Molly also talked about the clitoris, its function and form, and also about masturbation, mentioning in context "manual stimulation." About thirty minutes later while Molly was discussing methods of birth control, Skip, brow furled and steeped in thought, raised his hand. "Excuse me," he asked inquisitively, "but how *does* one manually stimulate the clitoris?"

At this point in her recitation Molly is chuckling uncontrollably from the back of her throat, hand held over her mouth. "I was so close to losing it, guys," she says, falling out in laughter along with the others.

The stories keep coming. One features a young man who performs condom demonstrations for health classes as part of a Peer-to-Peer program, then gets a young woman pregnant sans contraception several months later. Another is about a puckish student—"A little reprobate!" someone interjects—with wide-set eyes who once was suspended for stealing a laptop.

It's a rejuvenating if vaguely guilt-inducing lunch. To outsiders they may have appeared callous, unsympathetic, even cruel. But teachers are with their students for so many hours each week, observe so many of their interactions, and get to know them so well that moments of mockery are inevitable. And these moments can be difficult to keep to one's self.

Your work experience may not be wholly dissimilar. You've undoubtedly blathered about coworkers, bosses, and patrons. While the first two are risky given the potential to damage ongoing relationships, though certainly not uncommon, the latter feels somehow more innocuous. Clients, customers, and consumers seem to occupy a space beyond the professional divide, members of another group set apart from collegial fraternities, and prattling about them is normal. The relevant question is one of propriety.

Here two different parallels offer insight. First, the law. When attorneys and judges are in public it's customary to use first names only, which makes sense. If you're going to talk about individuals, whether they're clients or competitors, it's okay provided there's a modicum of anonymity. Naturally, first names are more common than family names so it's possible to refer to people with clarity while simultaneously cloaking their identity. This balances competing interests, weighing one's right to discuss work against the need to keep others from hearing about it.

The same is true, though to a different degree, in medicine. If you've ever known a nurse you may be fortunate enough to have been regaled with entertaining stories about patients: a sweet if repetitive grandmother with dementia, an annoying architect with gastrointestinal complications, a homeless alcoholic reciting impromptu poetry. Except nurses never mention their patients' names, not even their given ones. You can ask but they won't say—something about their allegiance to the Hippocratic oath—which is a nice equilibrium, trash talking troublesome patients while also categorically respecting their right to privacy.

In a similar way, teachers should be able to converse about their students. It's okay to gossip as long as they remain unaware. It's also fine to use students' full names around colleagues, though with outsiders first names, as is protocol in the legal world, should suffice. And since teachers spend much of their careers alone in a room of young people, the time and space to vent with other adults becomes sacred—like forty minutes with colleagues in your friend's classroom at lunch. Just be sure to shut the door.

Of course there are also times when openly messing with students is desirable. Building relationships is one of the most important keys to successful teaching and learning, and joking with students can be a good way of establishing a bond. The line between making a student feel comfortable versus embarrassed, however, is thin. If you're going to kid you must ensure students receive your teasing in the spirit in which it is given. Impact matters as much as, if not more than, intent. Because walking this line can be difficult, a high social intelligence is required of good teaching.

If you want to play it safe it's best not to discuss physical appearance. But what happens if a student has a fresh haircut and you want to tell her it looks nice? Or you're wearing the same shoes as a student and you want to compliment him, maybe razz him because yours are cleaner, your sneaker game tighter than his? How about when a student walks into your room with a black-and-white-striped blouse and all you want to tell her is she's just received a fifteen-yard personal foul and she'll need to back out of class and into the hall and try again wearing something slightly less ridiculous? Better save that one for lunch.

Or let's say a particular student has shared his research paper with you digitally so you're able to monitor his screen in real time as he's working. You look up and see him straight-faced, earnestly typing away. Evidently he forgets you can see his paper and following his introductory paragraph, because he is distracted or bored or procrastinating, he is writing:

Penis penis penis penis penis penis penis penis penis penis penis penis penis penis PENIS PENIS PENIS penis penis penis penis penis penis penis penis penis penis penis penis penis penises penis penis penis penis penis penis penis penis penis penis penis penis penis penis penises penis penis penis penis.

And so on for nearly two pages. You call his name and at this moment he's not entirely sure he has been caught. He makes the long walk to your desk and you turn your computer screen to show him the evidence. Do you shame him? Do you project his work on the big screen for the entire class to enjoy? Of course not. You read his face, slack-jawed, eyes glazed and distant, complexion pale as if on the verge of tearing up or fainting, and you decide to give him the silent treatment like parents who don't yell and scream when you've done something wrong and now you know they're really pissed.

You just nod and say, "Okay," and motion with your eyes for him to return to his seat. He doesn't move, his feet are glued to the floor, so you say it again. "*Okay.*" After a third time, he awakens and stumbles to his desk. You're laughing on the inside, not least because you're in the middle of the sex ed unit and you wonder what the heck is going through this teenager's mind. You don't even look at him when he leaves the room but as soon as class ends you rush to your colleague next door and show her his phallic treatise. Then you tell the lunchroom about it the next day, with the door closed, to howling laughter.

Is this appropriate teacher conduct? Certainly. The point is it's fine to make fun of students, or talk about them in any less-than-serious manner, as long as they don't know. It's also okay and sometimes even beneficial to tease students. It establishes a rapport and shows them you care. The key is knowing your students well enough to understand the difference between building them up and tearing them down, between creating relationships and destroying them.

Though Rob desperately wanted to call out Jenna for looking like a referee, he suspected she was too shy and sensitive to find it amusing. Regardless of how hard Molly wanted to laugh when her student asked, upon deep reflection, just how *did* one manually stimulate the clitoris, she refrained, buried it deep, saved it for the lunchroom. And surely it takes significant willpower not to call out your student for his compendium of penises, to ask him if you can save it as a model for future classes, or tell him it's so good his parents would love to receive a copy.

Interactions like these are standard fare, moments teachers encounter regularly, and they are analogous to behavior across many professions. Your own career experience is likely comparable: the indecorous stories about people for whom you might serve, represent, or care, can breathe life into a homespun routine, they can recharge your battery, let you blow off steam or come up for air.

Though it may feel painful to accept, this is also true of teachers. Yes, they love their students. They care about them deeply. And, from time to time, they also love making fun of them.

KEY IDEAS

- It's important to foster strong relationships with students, but a fine line exists between building teenagers up and breaking them down.
- Though there's an inclination in education to poke fun at students or gossip about them, it's best to do so in private with colleagues, family, or friends.

Chapter 29

Funeral for a Fallen Player

James and Tony are cousins who teach art and Spanish and coach their high school's basketball team. Recently a metropolitan police officer fatally wounded one of their former players named Carl "Bird" Andrews. After fleeing a vehicle, Carl allegedly brandished a pistol and was fired upon. Lawyers have raised questions about Carl's death and the shooting is being investigated but there's been no finding of wrongdoing.

Today James and Tony are attending Carl's funeral at Trinity Church in a northwestern neighborhood of the city underneath the shadows of a football stadium. Surrounded by Carl's mostly African American friends and family, James and Tony make up half the white people in attendance.

A coterie of what appear to be ministers, deacons, and preachers lead the service. Several people testify on Carl's soft-spoken, playful demeanor and someone recalls his beautiful singing voice. When a young relative no more than eight years old intones "His Eye Is on the Sparrow" there's hardly a dry eye in church.

Toward the end of the memorial, a processional is formed down the aisle, through the pews, to the open casket. The cousins haven't seen Carl since his graduation several years prior, and walking past his body they confront a near-unrecognizable face, heavily powdered and set in a twisted expression. It's not the young man they once knew.

James and Tony walk into the sunlight, commiserate for a while outside, then head for their truck. Along the way, three young women from the funeral eye them sharply. They exchange hellos and the young women compliment James and Tony's suits.

Then one woman asks, "You guys detectives or something?"

This is not the first time the cousins have been mistaken for police in a largely black neighborhood. Clean-cut and somewhat athletic, perhaps they fit the stereotype.

"No, we were Carl's coaches," Tony manages to say, though he wonders why the three women didn't see them as teachers, coworkers, or friends.

Against the backdrop of an enduring nationwide conversation about profiling and race, this is a telling moment. It illustrates that in order to move beyond snap judgments and see human beings instead of merely their labels, one must get to know people of different backgrounds.

And the best way to learn about different people is to *do* something with them. Israelis and Palestinians turning double plays; liberals and conservatives worshipping on Sunday; rich and poor football fans sharing a beer; gay and straight families celebrating a marriage; black and white kids completing school projects. One needs to see others for their true selves—instead of the many characteristics that incompletely define them.

James and Tony knew Carl because they shared the experiences of a team. Together they won, lost, sang over pasta dinners, and laughed at embarrassing plays. On a dark night at a quiet intersection, James and Tony might view another tattooed six-foot-six black man as a potential adversary in the same way those three girls saw the cousins as cops. However, since James and Tony have meaningful relationships with young African American men through teaching and coaching, they're less likely to judge other young African American men as criminals simply because of their appearance.

The extension of this argument is greater integration and diversity. It's the only way to truly, existentially, understand one another. After all, as many liberals will secretly admit, intellectualizing open-mindedness and living it are two very different things.

Sadly, what happened to Carl "Bird" Andrews may remain a mystery. Those three young women may not know any white men who aren't cops, and some individuals may not know a black man who isn't threatening.

But know this: until people see others for who they really are, which can only be accomplished through meaningful interactions with groups they don't know, our society will never be blind to difference in its many forms. And parents like Carl's will continue to bury their young.

KEY IDEAS

- Knowing people with different backgrounds makes it easier to see the humanity in all.
- The best way to understand a person is by doing something with him or her; and coaching and playing high-school sports provides an ideal opportunity for this to occur.

Chapter 30

Why Jessie Should
Attend Pomona Pitzer

Jessie, lingering one day after class, asks Leila to write her a letter of recommendation for college. Leila doesn't think twice. Says she'd be happy to.

Because Leila has been teaching freshman and an upper-division environmental science elective, she's been somewhat lucky. She's only assumed a small portion of the faculty's letter-writing burden.

As a practical matter, writing letters of recommendation falls most heavily on the shoulders of junior and senior teachers, especially the former. Since many applications are due in January at the beginning of the second semester, students prefer to ask junior teachers who previously taught them for an entire year and who possess an array of knowledge about their abilities. This often precludes senior teachers still acquainting themselves with their students in October and November when the letter of rec campaign is heating up.

Freshman and sophomore teachers, while available, are often passed over because students believe their more recent work is superior, and fear freshman and sophomore teachers won't adequately remember them, thus producing inferior recommendations. This is not to say freshman, sophomore, and senior teachers aren't called upon to write letters, only that junior teachers carry a disproportionate share of the load—an arbitrary and unfair consequence of teaching a particular grade.

Leila has been lucky because only first-semester seniors in environmental science, like Jessie, ask her for letters. Writing letters of rec is both time-intensive and a not-so-subtle form of volunteerism. Many efficient teachers and counselors claim they're able to write a letter in under an hour though this is hard to do: a thoughtful, polished letter takes closer to two. Though counselors are contractually required to write letters of rec as part of their job description, an enormous yearly undertaking for scores if not hundreds of students, teachers have discretion over how many letters they decide to write.

Teaching has a Sisyphean character to begin with, it's never quite possible to finish planning, assessing, giving feedback, and providing additional instruction, so you're never really done—you just decide to press pause for moments at a time. Add to this letter-writing season and it's understandable why some teachers have a strict protocol and often a cap. Limits might reach ten, twenty, even thirty letters. But by chance, because of the classes Leila's teaching, she's not asked for recommendations very often.

Several days after Jessie's request, she drops off a packet with some supporting documents. Leila realizes Jessie's letter is not due for a couple months so she sets a reminder and forgets about it. Jessie's is her first letter of the year and Leila presumes she has ample time. With three weeks before the deadline, and several other recommendation requests trickling in along the way, Leila begins considering what she wants to say about Jessie. She tries to think of a few words that described her—since Leila will be asked this question on Jessie's application anyway—and then use those words as the structure of her letter.

In truth, Leila is procrastinating.

She oscillates between assuring herself the letter doesn't mean much and suspecting, in fact, it actually does. As part of students' college application, in addition to test scores and grade point averages, students must secure letters of recommendation from several teachers and their counselor. Some say these letters are quite impactful, that they can be the deciding factor for admittance or rejection, while others believe admissions boards barely read them—especially if the student is clearly a Yes or a No.

About a week into procrastinating, Leila finally sits down and completes a draft. She describes Jessie as principled, grounded, analytical, and says these are her reasons for recommending Jessie "for admittance to your institution." Though the counselor's letter of rec paints a broader picture of the student, whereas teachers' letters are designed to articulate academic potential through classroom experience, Jessie is a special person and Leila wants to mention why, to discuss Jessie's heart before transitioning to her head.

Leila relates a story of Jessie helping a special needs student one day after class to illustrate her virtue, and another showing how her upbringing in a small town, a forty-five-minute commute over serpentine, breathtaking, cliff-hugging roads, has developed in her a high social intelligence and maturity beyond her years.

But presuming her counselor will flesh out Jessie's character more fully, Leila devotes the bulk of her letter to examining Jessie's academic ability. Fortunately, Jessie is a student about whom Leila has much to say and she struggles keeping her letter to one single-spaced page—the recommended standard. (For other students, reaching the end of a page feels like a marathon distance.)

To portray Jessie as an analytical thinker, Leila recounts a recent lesson in which Jessie showed a sophisticated capacity to analyze disparate facts and express their relationship to the process of natural selection.

At the end of the letter Leila attempts to bring it all together. *In sum, in addition to Jessie's principled character and grounded personality, it is because of her analytical mind that I am writing to express my deep, heartfelt support of Jessie for admittance to your institution. She will think, she will learn, and she will make you proud.*

Then Leila buries the draft for a few days before looking at it anew with fresh eyes, some distance, and a sense of calm (putting words on the page is always Leila's most difficult step, whereas revising she finds much easier and sometimes even pleasurable). In addition to fixing errant typos Leila varies the syntax here and there and replaces several vague words with more specific ones. The foundation of the letter is solid; she just needs to scrub it down, polish it up, make it pretty.

While Leila doesn't have a letter-writing template per se, she does follow a general construction: she'll say something like *I am writing to express my deepest support of [So and So] for admittance to your institution.* Sometimes she'll vary the modifiers like "deepest," "heartfelt," or "sincere," and sometimes she won't include any modifiers at all depending on how she feels about the particular student.

Then Leila will lay down a background sentence or two about her relationship to the applicant, finishing the first paragraph with the adjectives she'll be using throughout the letter (principled, grounded, analytical). In the body, she'll illustrate each descriptor with an anecdote to show what she's trying to tell, to provide concrete context for her abstract assessment so the reader can at least glimpse the student in action (special needs student, natural selection).

Leila will also say something quirky or unexpected or even slightly off-color to jolt the readers from their miasma, a quick "Hey, look at this!" to disrupt the monotony and make sure they're paying attention (Odyssean commute). Then she'll close with a line similar to the introduction, adjusting her support based on her feelings for the student ("deep," "heartfelt").

Perhaps this is a template after all. College letters of recommendation are not free-flowing, enthymematic personal essays. Leila wants to write engagingly but also concisely, with clarity and precision. At least she's not recycling sentences or paragraphs or entire letters, inserting one student's name for another—though the temptation is understandable, especially since some teachers based purely on their grade-level and subject area are called upon to write tens of letters each year.

Leila sits on Jessie's letter another day then reads it over a third time to be extra certain it's game-ready. Fortunately, the application process is now digitized. Instead of printing letters for multiple schools on proper stationery, signing them, folding them into thirds, sticking them in official envelopes, writing each university's name on the front cover of those envelopes, stamping, licking, and finally sealing them, Leila just clicks submit. Done and done.

As it happens, Leila sees Jessie the following day in class. "Guess what? Finished your letter," Leila says and extends her knuckles for a triumphant bump.

"Oh wow, thanks!"

"You bet."

When it's all said and done, how does Leila know if she's written a good letter? Sure she could examine models from respected colleagues and research letter-writing advice, but she's never received any feedback—and most teachers won't either. Writing letters of rec is an ancillary endeavor many teachers do without much guidance, maybe even much reflection. There's no course one must complete as part of a teacher credentialing program—Letters of Rec 101 does not exist—and the subject is hardly discussed among faculties let alone the larger community. Rarely is it mentioned in professional-development seminars or teacher contracts.

But college letters of recommendation have the potential to be extremely consequential in the lives of students. Admissions boards generally review GPAs, test scores, letters of rec, and anything else included in an application. So what teachers write is enormously impactful, and usually done gratis by those who believe it's the right thing to do. If each letter takes at minimum one hour to compose, and a teacher writes fifteen letters, that's nearly two extra days of work. And some teachers write considerably more, perhaps double or triple that amount, such as those teaching juniors or English. Goodbye nights and weekends.

Two days later, Jessie stays once again after class, this time to hand Leila an envelope of her own. When Jessie leaves Leila opens it and finds a thank-you card with a bird on the cover and a handwritten message inside. The thank you only reinforces Leila's warm feelings for Jessie.

Unfortunately, notes like Jessie's are the exception rather than the rule, and perhaps students just don't know any better. After all, it can be easy to forget teachers are people. So for anyone who may someday request a letter of recommendation here's a tip: say thank you. Write a thank-you note. You don't need to include anything else—all teachers really want is your appreciation. Trust that it will mean a lot. Your teacher may even keep your note for posterity in a file cabinet by her desk.

It's impolitic to say, of course, so on behalf of all those too proud or too polite to express how they truly feel: students, teachers will write your letters of recommendation. Though it might seem like they have more pressing tasks to accomplish, like your letters are their version of homework, they'll write them, eventually, because they care about you and your future success.

In exchange, please write them a thank-you note. It doesn't have to be much and it needn't cost a penny. Inscribe a few handwritten sentences on a small card or piece of paper. Place the paper in an envelope. Give your teachers the pleasure of opening the envelope and discovering your kind words. They will grant your teachers strength, energy to write the next letter.

You don't even have to include a gift card.

KEY IDEAS

- Letters of recommendation are essential for students; and though they take some time to complete and may feel like extra work, even volunteer work, teachers will gladly write them.
- As a sign of their appreciation, students should give teachers a thank-you note.

Chapter 31

Thinking about Jae

Dave has been thinking a lot recently about JaeShon. This week JaeShon has seemed pretty down. Dave is aware of what's going on but he doesn't want to bring it up every time they see each other, so Dave just grins and says What's up, Jae! and tries to appear friendly and open.

Tonight Dave sees Jae at the basketball game. Everyone in the student section is cheering and joking and palling around but Jae seems removed, reserved, distant. They make eye contact once from across the stands but when Dave tries to throw him a head nod Jae quickly looks away.

Though Jae is usually a happy-go-lucky kid, some of his joy has abated. His smiles have become fewer and less bright. Dave remembers reading a profile about Jae's football prowess in the local newspaper and learning "Smiley" has been his family nickname since he was young. See that's the thing, family. Jae's had a tough go of it. He lives with his grandma because his mom is absent, allegedly staying several towns away. While his grandma's great, a grandmother is a difficult substitute for a mom. And then there's his dad, the reason Jae has been dejected of late. His dad has been in jail for over two years.

In a strange way, this misfortune is what brought Jae and Dave closer together. Dave taught Jae as a sophomore in Academic Workshop, an elective offering extra tutoring and support. Because many of the kids in Academic Workshop were arriving hungry, Dave starts filling the back cabinet with snacks: first candy then granola bars.

At some point Dave notices Jae never eats the granola bars and after a while he asks him why. They hurt my teeth, Jae says. Since AW is the last period of the day Dave often grows hungry himself, and occasionally he'll dip into his leftover pretzels from lunch. Eventually he offers some to Jae and he says yes, then asks about them the following class, so Dave starts packing him an extra bag.

This year Jae is enrolled in Dave's Government class. The granola bars are long devoured and, to be honest, Dave has forgotten about their pretzel pact until one day before class Jae says No pretzels? in this way he does when his voice rises in pitch and inflection. So now they're continuing the tradition.

Dave doesn't make a big deal about it, he just places the pretzels at the end of his desk and sooner or later Jae comes and grabs them. A few times the empty bag hasn't returned—Jae says because he's been sharing with other people and they throw it away—and Dave will razz him about the benefits of "reduce, reuse, recycle." If I'm reusing the same bag every day, Dave tells him, then so can Jae.

Anyway, enough about pretzels. Lately Jae has been low because his dad is in jail and now it's looking like he's going to be there for a long time. It's not until this year that Dave learns his dad is incarcerated in the first place. They're talking about the difference between prison and jail—the former implying a year or more behind bars and the latter a year or less—when Jae raises his hand, something he rarely does. No, that's not right, he says, because my dad is in jail and he's been there for over two years.

His comment hits Dave like a ton of bricks. There's something stark about the way he says it, not nonchalantly but so matter-of-fact. Dave fumbles through an explanation of a new law that has reduced penalties for certain crimes and means some inmates traditionally held in prison are now being transferred to county jails. I'm really sorry to hear that, Dave manages to say at least, before his halting explanation is complete.

After class Dave asks Jae more about his dad. That's when he learns his dad is in jail not due to the new law but, because he can't make his two-million-dollar bail, that he's being held this whole time prior to trial. Since booking logs are public knowledge, they look up Jae's dad's case and the charges against him. They're numerous, some quite violent. Jae and Dave chat for a while longer and at some point Jae walks away. When Jae leaves, Dave searches online for stories about Jae's dad and talks with several school employees, who live nearby and know the family, for more context.

In part because the curriculum seems relevant to his dad's case, Jae begins stopping by Dave's room to talk. Maybe he also sees Dave as a guy who played sports, and therefore someone he can respect. In addition to telling Dave how many touchdowns he scores, yards he runs, and passes he catches, Jae starts revealing more about his life. He speaks about being handcuffed multiple times while hanging with his buddies, including once when he and his flat-topped friend were "roasted" by the police for resembling Kid 'n Play.

He also tells Dave about lying in bed at night and hearing gunshots. Like probably once a week, he says, after Dave interrupts him. Jae explains he peeks through the curtains above his bed to see what's going on, though he doesn't really need to because he can sense from the sound what's what. A bunch of pops in a row—pop-pop-pop-pop-pop—means someone's just firing his gun into the air for fun. But if he hears one pop, then a pause, then a few more—pop, pop-pop—that means someone is shooting at someone else.

I can tell, Jae says, I just get this weird feeling from the sounds and I know something bad is happening. Dave wants to ask how Jae lives like that, how he's able to sleep or relax or do homework, how he can focus on anything at all, but Dave doesn't. Dave wants to tell Jae that Dave's unsure if he's ever heard a gunshot in his life.

Jae also gives Dave updates about his dad's next court appearance, about preliminary motions and rumors of a potential plea. And for a while there appears to be good reason for hope: from what Dave can gather through the public booking log and Jae's conversations with his dad, the district attorney seems to be delaying, putting things off, raising new issues. All of which seems like good news.

They don't have anything *on* him! Jae keeps saying. He tells Dave about exculpatory security camera footage, conflicting witness testimony, and a lack of forensic evidence. Jae even skips several classes to drive with his older brother—both of whose names are clever iterations of their dad's—to attend court proceedings.

As the wheels of justice turn slowly one month bleeds into another. Jae earns better than a 3.0 G.P.A. his first semester and, along with it, a burrito from his counselor. Dave is insanely impressed with the kid. Star football player, anchor of the 400-meter relay team, honor roll, glowing smile. Attending several of Jae's football games Dave tells his grandma how highly he thinks of Jae. And though Dave understands his mom's not around, Dave also knows Jae still communicates with his dad.

So one day Dave mentions to Jae that sometimes he calls home to talk with the parents of kids who are doing particularly well—not just those faring poorly—and that Dave would love to speak with Jae's dad, tell him how he feels, how proud Dave is of Jae and his accomplishments, but Dave doesn't know if it's possible given his dad's situation.

All right, Jae says, concealing a smile then looking down at his phone. In the afternoon Jae returns to inform Dave people can't call into the jail, you have to wait for someone inside to contact you, but that he'll have his dad get in touch during the school day sometime so he and Dave can chat. Maybe during tutorial would be good, Dave says.

The following Friday morning Jae comes to Dave's room and tells him his dad is going to call around 10:00. Perfect, Dave says, that's during the rally so we should be able to talk. When tutorial begins Dave walks with his class to the gym and as students scatter into the stands he finds a few teacher friends by the exit, only half remembering the arrangement. Out of the corner of his eye Dave notices Jae standing alongside the bleachers rather than sitting with his friends. Jae keeps thumbing his phone and peeking at Dave. Dave checks his phone too, sees the time is 9:50, and figures it out.

As the hour nears, Jae begins looking at his phone and at Dave with greater frequency, and Dave feels a tinge of nervous excitement himself. But then 10:00 becomes 10:10, 10:20, 10:30. The whole time Jae and Dave never make direct eye contact but Dave can feel Jae's disappointment. Not wanting to exacerbate an already uncomfortable moment, Dave doesn't approach Jae. Instead, when the rally ends he leaves the gym with his teacher friends and returns to his room, figuring he'll see Jae soon enough. Though Jae is supposed to be in Government the next period, he never shows up.

On Monday Dave waits until after class to ask him what happened. Oh, there was a lockdown, Jae says as if it were no big deal, so he wasn't able to call. Dave plays along. Okay, he says casually, let's try again sometime. Weeks pass and Dave never speaks with Jae's dad. Maybe they both forget, or maybe neither of them want to make new plans for fear of a similar result.

Then Jae stops by Dave's room to tell him Bryan Stevenson, founder of the Equal Justice Initiative, who Dave has recently mentioned in class, is going to be speaking at the convention center about his work exonerating the wrongfully imprisoned. No way, Dave exclaims, I want to go! and he immediately begins searching for tickets. Jae says he thinks the event is sold out but that he's going with a community group. Dave says he's jealous and makes Jae promise to let him know how it goes.

The next day Jae stops by Dave's room after school. He says he attended what turned out to be a book talk. Afterward he stood in line and, when it was his turn, recounted his dad's story to Mr. Stevenson, who responded by giving Jae his card and telling Jae to send him an email with more details. Great! Dave says. Have you written him yet? No, Jae replies. You have to do it, man! Why not? Dave says. Well I'm not exactly sure what to say, Jae says. Then he pauses.

Think you could help me?

Dave's heart swells.

Yeah, let's do it. They talk it over and Dave asks Jae some questions to get his mind working, nudge him in the right direction. Eventually Jae begins speaking as Dave types at his computer. He's paraphrasing, putting Jae's ideas into sentences Dave thinks are clear and encapsulate what Jae's trying to say. At the end Dave includes a postscript so everything is on the up-and-up.

Dear Mr. Stevenson,

It was nice meeting you this Tuesday at your book talk. If you remember me, I approached you on behalf of my father, who is going to be sentenced for several felonies including assault with a deadly weapon, burglary, robbery, and false imprisonment of a hostage.

I want to tell you that we had a public defender and that didn't go well. Then we paid for a lawyer and in my personal opinion I think it's "iffy." I'm not very confident in the job he is doing.

I believe my dad's arrest and trial are unfair because they're going off his past and not what he has been arrested for. My dad already did three years. He was arrested and has been in jail ever since because we cannot afford the two-million-dollar bail. They only have circumstantial evidence. Also, I believe the jail he's being held in is a pretty prejudiced place.

I remember you talked about hope and how you're never supposed to lose it. Well, everyone, including my dad and all my family, has lost hope. But not me.

I am wondering if you would be willing to help my dad. Whatever you can do. I know you probably get a lot of these types of emails but you never know. I just know I am not going to lose hope. And you are my hope.

Sincerely,
Jae
P.S. Just to let you know, I'm writing this with the help of my teacher.

Dave prints a copy for Jae and emails him a draft so he can send it. When Jae finishes reading his face lights up for a brief moment. Thanks, he says, and walks out. Let me know when you hear back, Dave says. I will, Jae calls out over his shoulder.

After Jae leaves, Dave thinks about Jae's life and his own. Jae's dad is in his midthirties, Dave remembers, not much older than him. Dave grew up not far from Jae's hometown but it might as well have been a world apart. If Jae's dad and Dave had switched places, experienced alternate upbringings, would their current situations be reversed as well?

Dave could be the one incarcerated, father of a teenage son. He wonders what life would be like for Jae with a mother and father who were always there, who watched his football games and track meets and celebrated his stellar report cards. Dave doesn't know how else to say it except that life seems really unfair.

Months pass and one day Jae walks in to tell Dave that while he hasn't heard back from Mr. Stevenson he does have other news: his dad is taking a plea. He's agreed to twelve years, minus nearly three for time served, so he'll be in eight, and soon he'll be moved from the county jail to upstate prison. This time—again—Dave doesn't have a great response. About all he can muster is I'm sorry, that at least his dad has been credited with time served and he'll be out soon. Dave wishes he'd told him something else.

Needless to say, the past few days have been hard on Jae. Outwardly he appears to be coping, though he doesn't stop by as often so Dave isn't really sure. Then tonight Dave spots him at the basketball game and Jae quickly looks away. He turns to his friends and puts on a genial expression, a mask of something deeper. Dave wonders if seeing him brought up feelings Jae's been trying to avoid.

Tonight Dave is thinking about Jae and his heart is at once full and broken. Jae has so many things going for him, so many cards stacked against him. Regardless of the plea bargain, if the letter works and Mr. Stevenson takes the case and exonerates Jae's dad there's a screenplay in it: the son who rescues his father. But that would be Hollywood—this is real life.

There are other ways for Jae to be a superhero though. He can graduate from high school and go to college and get a meaningful job, lead a meaningful existence. For a young man like Jae to succeed, to rise from a poor, nonnuclear family in a community that has faced historic discrimination, sometimes Dave thinks that would be nothing short of superheroic. A Hollywood ending in its own right.

Dave is thinking about Jae saying everyone else has given up hope but that he'll never give up on his dad. He's thinking about a kid for whom he cares deeply, and about what it's going to take for him to make it. Jae, Dave wants to tell him, I haven't given up on you either.

KEY IDEAS

- Teachers occasionally form extra-special relationships with students.
- When these students struggle, or are living with unfair disadvantages, there's no end to the lengths teachers want to go to help.

Chapter 32

The Sheepdog and the Wolf

You may remember as a kid watching Merrie Melodies cartoons about an anthropomorphic sheepdog and wolf. They would eat breakfast together, walk together to work, arrive simultaneously at a red time clock.

"Morning, Ralf."

"Morning, Sam."

Though friends, upon punching in the two became dueling adversaries perpetually concocting schemes to foil the other's plans. Sam, flop of rusty hair draped over his eyes, would attempt to prohibit Ralf, the Wile E. Coyote doppelgänger with a Rudolph-red nose, from capturing and presumably devouring members of Sam's flock. Ralf's tactics were madcap and diverse: he would lasso, dive-bomb, fishhook, and impersonate sheep (a wolf in their clothing), launch missiles, set traps with hungry alligators, and unleash rabid Acme wildcats while Sam wasn't looking.

Yet Sam always thwarted Ralf's efforts; he would materialize atop the tunnel, swing a larger lasso, mimic the sheep Ralf was conspiring to apprehend. Always cool, Sam never raised his voice or lost his temper, never grew annoyed at his rival's antics, taking them all in stride. Not that Ralf escaped punishment—Sam wasn't above pounding him with a mallet, flattening him with a severed section of cliff, or saddling him with sticks of quick-fuse dynamite.

But perhaps the most memorable moments occurred at the end of their collective shifts. No matter how antagonistically they may have acted toward one another during the day, they were civil. Sam and Ralf might be seconds away from mortal combat, rockets target-locked, blades sharpened to a razor edge, but when the whistle sounded they froze, suspended their skirmishes to begin anew the following morning.

"That's good for today, Ralf."

145

"Okay, Sam. I guess you can't win 'em all."

And together they would leave the field of battle walking side by side over the horizon and into the sunset.

In Ritchie's first year teaching he often feels like Sam the Sheepdog. Especially with a student whose name is Luke. Ritchie and Luke have some experience, going back to when Luke was an elementary schooler at a music camp where Ritchie worked for many years.

It quickly becomes evident their relationship has changed from the summer camps of yore. As a young teacher, Ritchie's been having difficulty beginning classes; if he doesn't set the tone and start with complete student focus, he'll be playing catch-up the rest of the way. With Luke's period he tries everything—pausing, staring, calling students out, plowing ahead, writing names on the board, raising his voice—and through it all Luke sits upright in the front row wearing a large grin. He's smart enough to be quiet yet also savvy enough to know once the room settles down is precisely his moment to strike.

"Any questions?" Ritchie asks after finally getting the class' attention and previewing the lesson for the day.

On cue Luke raises his hand. "Did you hear about that car crash last night?" and class spirals out of control while Luke attempts to wrest it back. When Ritchie eventually stops calling on him Luke doubles down. "No, this is serious," he says with an up-nod and a smirk, "I really want to talk about what the president said yesterday. It's relevant, I swear." On rare occasions it is.

Luke toys with Ritchie in other ways. One day Ritchie has just distributed their first test, after a night of tweaking, proofreading, agonizing over each question, and he's scanning the room for signs of rebellion or befuddlement. When Luke looks up from his paper Ritchie assumes he's uncovered a mistake, a typo or ambiguity or mix-up in numbering.

"Good test," he says.

It's a Vince Vaughn line from the film *Old School*. In possession of the answers during an elaborate cheating conspiracy, Vaughn, the consummate smartass, whispers "Good test" to his college professor with a charming mix of sincerity and ridicule. Luke and Ritchie have swapped movie quotes before, at seventeen and twentysomething they're both in the prime of their movie-quoting years, and Luke's delivery is pitch-perfect. Ritchie still chuckles recalling the likeness of Luke's rendition (though in hindsight he wonders if Luke was telling Ritchie he already had the answers).

Despite the consequences, Luke hunts for laughter with a single-mindedness. The class funny man, he feeds off his peers' energy and sometimes just can't resist. The following semester, for example, they're debating the constitutional limits of free speech on campus and Ritchie is enjoying a rare new-teacher moment with active student participation and a high level of involvement. When Luke raises his hand Ritchie is thrilled, only to hear

Luke utter an obscene phrase with several different formulations of "fuck." The class strikes up a whoop and instinctively looks to Ritchie for his reaction as Ritchie tries to keep a straight face.

He can't—even though he's kind of pissed.

"You're lucky that's funny," Ritchie says, chuckling against his will.

It's unclear why Ritchie finds Luke so amusing. For one reason or another, Luke makes him laugh. *Good test.* Though they're several years apart, in another context they could be friends, and maybe it's simply a matter of their different roles, Luke the student and Ritchie the teacher.

Which is not unlike a certain sheepdog and wolf. One can picture Luke spending his morning tiptoeing through the classroom, stalking jokes, waiting for his moment to pounce, while Ritchie struggles dutifully to catch him. Surely there are occasions when Luke's humor becomes a hindrance and Ritchie wants to thump him over the head, shove him off a cliff, strap him on a rocket ship to the moon.

But Ritchie would do well to channel Sam's nonchalant vigilance. When it comes to corralling students, to redirecting their focus and keeping them on task, Ritchie might emulate Sam by not getting worked up, beaten down, or bent out of shape. If Sam wants to keep his flock safe, Ritchie wants to ensure his is learning.

As the years pass, teachers' relationships with their students evolve but it's still helpful thinking in cartoons. Like Bugs Bunny and Yosemite Sam, teachers and students need not be adversaries, nor best-of-friends like Bugs Bunny and Daffy Duck. Instead they might resemble Porky and his young mentee Hamton J. Pig.

Envision the blue-overalled, lop-eared Hamton attending Acme Looniversity under the tutelage of his favorite teacher Porky. They spend their time at Acme studying the looniverse, thinking about what it means to be a pig, contemplating the nature of their porcine existence.

As class finishes the curtains descend and a familiar melody rises: *daaa-da-da-da, da-da-da-da, da-da-da-da . . . Da-da-da-da, da-daaaaaaaaa!* And Porky, in his trademark stutter, wishes Hamton and his classmates farewell, to learn together another day.

Th-th-th-that's all, folks!

KEY IDEA

- Students and teachers often have different relationships in and out of the classroom.

Section VI

MORE THAN A
CLASSROOM TEACHER

Chapter 33

Sibling Tricycle Grudge Match

High-school pep rallies. You've been there, you've seen them, you know what they're like. Whether a recent grad or distant alum, you probably have a fair grasp of their nature. They still feature chest-bumping varsity athletes, homecoming courts, and gobs of saccharine school spirit. And though you may have fond or uncomfortable or even wildly entertaining memories, it is doubtful any of them involve the adults who oversaw the rallies at all.

For most teachers these events matter very little. They are required to attend and supervise. They monitor the audience for signs of mischief like mistakenly exposed contraband, clandestinely launched projectiles, and impromptu chants of "Fresh-men." If possible, teachers prefer to stand by the rear exit or atop the amphitheater as far removed from the action as possible. Indeed, rally supervision may be the least effort teachers put into, and the least thought they give about, their jobs.

Unless, of course, you're a rookie. In which case you'll be made to participate in some humbling public initiation not much different from the fate of freshman students themselves. You'll grin and bear it because as a first- or second-year teacher it's important to ingratiate yourself with staff and especially the administration.

This means when members of the associated student body's rally-coordinating team email the faculty soliciting volunteers for the lip sync or dance contest you are unofficially obliged to acquiesce. And if that's all you're made to do you're getting off easy. At least you didn't enter the dunk tank. Or race your sibling in a tricycle relay of death.

Consider brothers Austin and Reed. Austin has been teaching English for several years when Reed is hired to coach basketball and teach PE. In many ways, teaching and coaching with his little brother is an unrecognized dream come true for Austin. It brings them closer together. (And though Austin

151

cannot know at the time how soon Reed will be gone, following his heart to the ranks of college coaching and, Austin secretly suspects, because PE teachers aren't held in especially high regard, their three years as colleagues will be the happiest of Austin's career.)

Mostly it's fun hearing students talk about them, getting asked who's older, what it's like teaching together, and who's the better athlete—who can beat whom in any variety of physical pursuits. One day their friend, the leadership teacher, decides it will be fun to find out in front of the entire school. With five years' separation between them, Austin and Reed are far enough apart that they never came in direct competition, which is to say at ten, fifteen, and twenty Austin could always beat his five-, ten- and fifteen-year-old brother at pretty much everything.

Except now Reed is entering their school only two years removed as captain of his collegiate basketball team while Austin hasn't played a sport competitively in years. At twenty-four, Reed has somehow turned the tables while Austin wasn't paying attention (though Austin would never admit it). So when Austin and Reed are approached to participate in what's being billed as a sibling obstacle course they give an enthusiastic yes—but quickly realize the stakes.

Two days before the event, they attend a rehearsal and after being informed of the relay format decide to ham it up for the crowd. On Friday, what seems like the entire school streams into the gym for the annual winter sports rally. The building is packed; students are spilling down the bleachers and onto the court.

One by one, the varsity sports teams break through paper banners, jumping up and down and gesticulating boldly. Several basketball players engage in a suburban dunk contest. After numerous missed attempts, one high-flyer successfully nudges the ball over the rim to a burst of overenthusiastic applause. Afterward, the wrestling team, blindfolded, plays musical chairs.

"And now, everybody, we have a special treat," the emcee says. "Today the Brothers are going to participate in a head-to-head competition!"

Reed and Austin step out from behind the stands, remove their jackets, and walk to mid-court. Along the way they notice their new superintendent seated near the sideline. Before anyone is ready, the emcee is explaining the rules and they're off.

"On-your-marks-get-set-go!"

Crammed into red kid-sized tricycles, they begin Flintstoning toward the opposite basket as the gym erupts in cheers. Like a seasoned older brother, Austin pushes Reed from his trike and shoots, or waddles, out to an early lead. In Reed's attempt to stay seated he pushes Austin forward and by some quirk of physics propels Austin into a standing position. As Austin's tricycle rolls slowly down the court he jumps with both feet on the seat, attempting to ghost ride it, surf it, to the opposite baseline. But he loses his balance and kicks out as the trike races away.

At this point Reed is trailing. Hunched with both arms over the handlebars, he runs his tricycle down the court, crashing into Austin as Austin attempts to rescue his from the stands. Then all hell breaks loose. As if they're kids wrestling in their shared bedroom, Reed lowers into a crouch and attempts to spear Austin. Austin sidesteps his brother's assault and in the sideways logic of a puppy, chases after him as Reed runs toward the free throw line.

But at some point mid-retreat, Reed spins, goes for Austin's knees, and takes him down. The crowd's screaming intensifies. They roll around until Reed lights off toward the starting line for the second leg of the relay, both of them ditching their tricycles and along with them the rules. Not to be outdone, Austin dives at Reed headfirst like a base stealer and wraps up his legs from behind. Reed lurches forward, smacking his chest and nearly his teeth against the floor. But they're still having fun.

After more tussling, grins on their faces and growing short of breath, they grab basketballs from an astonished leadership student and dribble back down the court. Reed pokes Austin's ball away, in the process losing his own, and as Reed does, Austin tackles him from behind by the shoulders, falling violently on top of him to the ground. They both pop up and search for their balls, knowing the first to score a basket will win. Austin locates his ball first and sprints toward the hoop.

With his ball nowhere in sight, Reed chases after him, steals Austin's ball as Austin is about to shoot, and tries to score himself—but Austin hacks at his arms and when they fall to the floor Austin lands on the ball and smothers it. Reed scrambles to his feet in search of the second basketball. On his back, Austin heaves an impossible if optimistic set shot that falls decidedly short. While Austin stands up, Reed grabs the rebound and valiantly attempts a reverse left-handed layup as Austin fouls and tackles him, yet again, to the floor. Reed's shot misses long off the backboard.

By now they're both dying of exhaustion, winded like the final rounds of a cage match, and the end will have to come soon. They chase after their basketballs and Austin finds one about fifteen feet away on the wing. He picks it up, steps back, and releases an arching jumper. Reaching its apex, it appears to descend on target. Then Austin notices Reed standing beneath the hoop with the other basketball in his hands.

As Austin's ball enters the rim Reed shoots his up through the net, blasting Austin's off the backboard and into the stands. Austin thinks he's won. He believes the ball has penetrated enough of the cylinder to count as it would in a real game. But this is no-holds-barred. Reed retrieves his ball, flips in a layup, and the crowd cheers. As they greet their team and the school mascot by the sideline Austin notices Reed is missing a shoe.

"Looks like we have a winner!" the emcee announces. Reed walks to mid-court, shoe in hand, and lowers his head in anticipation of receiving the celebratory medal. But Austin snatches it from the emcee, proclaims victory and then, feigning remorse, makes as if to award Reed the medal after all. As Reed lowers a second time Austin mock-knees his head, pushes it away, and keeps the medal for himself, the consummate older brother.

The violence of their exhibition is by all accounts astonishing. They never turn serious as with so many fraternal bouts but the spotlight is shining so they get after it, beat each other up, put on a show. One can imagine the superintendent's bewilderment at two brothers bashing themselves in an auditorium packed with teenagers.

Hopefully, Reed and Austin's display brings their campus a little closer together, gives students and faculty something to talk about. At their best, rallies can unite a school, strengthen bonds, and create feelings of a shared community. Everyone wants to belong, especially as adolescents, and rallies can imbue the school culture with a sense of positivity and an unspoken kindness. Maybe in some idealized way this is what Reed and Austin are trying to do (otherwise they're just being idiots).

At their worst, however, rallies can become pageants of the popular, opportunities for upperclassmen to demonstrate their status atop the social heap— whether this means acting up on center stage or tuning out in the back row. Rallies can perpetuate banal stereotypes and squeeze students into predefined roles: the jocks, the partiers, the misfits, the nerds and loners, and, of course, the dance team. Everyone must play a part; alternate identities are prohibited.

Sometimes rallies can also illuminate difficult truths. Sometimes they shine a light on hidden issues facing a school, one of the few times the entire student body assembles in one place. Sometimes the imagery is striking. Who participates, who sits where and with whom, and what this says about ethnicity, class and gender, about inequality and the achievement gap, can reveal more than words.

But mostly rallies are something about which teachers give very little thought. Just show up, don't let anyone do anything wildly inappropriate— like chug sweetened vodka behind the bleachers, in which case you'll have to apprehend the offenders and deliver them to the office—then return to your classroom and get on with your day. Teachers are required to supervise so that's what most of them do, though some renegades skip altogether, staying in their rooms to plan, grade, read the news.

Mostly these teachers won't miss much. Grade levels will execute class cheers, athletes will remind the audience they play sports, and some intrepid students will be summoned to perform embarrassing tasks in front of their peers. Rookie teachers, too, are especially at risk of school-wide humiliation, a charitable if institutionalized form of hazing. It might be a new-teacher lip synch or a dance-off or trivia game. Or a tricycle relay slugfest with your younger brother.

The next year Reed and Austin are supervising another rally. They're standing with their friends atop the amphitheater under a shining sun, putting forth minimal effort. The rally is like so many others—except this one features an inflatable jousting ring. Various combinations of students strap on face guards, climb up wobbly rotating pillars, grab oversize foam-padded lances like teenage American Gladiators, and battle for glory. After a while the crowd grows restless, tired of the spectacle. But time remains before sending students back to class and the emcee has to stall. He looks over at the leadership teacher, who whispers something in his ear.

"Before we let you go," the emcee calls out over the music, "we have one final surprise."

Reed and Austin should have seen it coming.

"Let's bring the Brothers down for another competition!"

They look at each other, shock quickly giving way to juvenile excitement, and bound down the aisle. They will settle matters once and for all.

KEY IDEAS

- For all that's changed over the decades in education, pep rallies have remained remarkably consistent, including how much (or little) teachers care about them.
- At best, rallies unite a high school; at worst, they divide it, reinforcing harmful stereotypes.
- Never battle your younger brother in front of teenagers—especially when pride is on the line.

Chapter 34

Staff Infections

Janet has just finished making copies and writing the agenda on the board for tomorrow when Maggie peeks her head into Janet's classroom.

"Let's go," Maggie says.

"Okay, right after I finish this email."

Janet closes the door behind her and they bump into another colleague headed in the opposite direction.

"Ready for the staff meeting?" Maggie asks him, clearly not ready herself.

"Yeah right," he responds. "Think we'll get anything done?"

The answer, most likely, is no.

With a minute to spare, Maggie and Janet file into the back door of the conference room. Discovering most teachers have occupied the back rows while a few have settled up front, they plop down along the far aisle of the thinly populated center. Behind them is a rookie art teacher. The soccer coach, a special-education teacher, slides over next to Maggie and Janet as school secretaries disperse raffle tickets to those who have arrived on time. An agenda is projected overhead.

After introductory remarks from their principal the meeting begins with a presentation from the student body president about a new hall pass system. Hall roaming has been a hot-button topic so instead of individualized passes—Janet's was a VCR tape ("Do you even know what this *is*?" she'd needle students)—now all teachers have color-coded lanyard cards: orange for bathroom, green for office, purple for teacher's assistant.

"They're sitting in your mailboxes as we speak!" the student body president says. "Any questions?" There are none; everyone claps and she smiles and leaves the room. Though having students write their name, date, and class period on the back of each pass every time they leave the room seems onerous, and may soon to be forgotten, it's worth a shot. Thank you, next topic.

The faculty then receives a fire drill update from an assistant principal. He reviews staff feedback following their recent exercise and promises to email the full results. The new routes and an additional staging area seem to have worked well, he says, noting that bottlenecking decreased around most entrances and exits.

"Any questions?"

None once again. Next topic.

They're already two bullets into the agenda and moving right along when another assistant principal stands to discuss attendance, truancy, and discipline. Too many kids in the halls has also meant too many kids arriving late to class, she says, announcing a new policy (which is actually the old policy of five years prior). She indicates students will now receive a detention after three tardies or unexcused absences or any combination thereof, and a suspension in severe cases upon multiple detentions. Seems like a solid adjustment. Next topic.

"Any questions?"

Several hands shoot up simultaneously. Teachers ask about potential losses of credit, how many tardies equals a detention, and where it will be held—most of which she has just explained. Then from the back of the room comes a lengthy soliloquy masquerading as a question expressing discomfort with the new rules. Emboldened by the monologue another teacher chimes in. "So are they going to do something in detention . . . or will it be like the Breakfast Club?"

Janet smirks at the soccer coach, looks around, and feels the audience begin to stir. Three teachers have put their heads in their hands, sitting eyes closed as if wishing they were anywhere else. Yet there are more questions: How will you inform students? What happens if they don't show? Isn't this just a prison system? Janet takes a deep breath. Eventually after several more comments one teacher raises her hand to thank the administration for the policy change and everyone claps. After a modest derailment it's time to get back on track. Next topic.

They begin to hear about a newly formed technology committee but before the English teacher who is presenting can finish, a familiar hand rises from the back of the room. Initially hesitant, the English teacher relents.

This time there is a protracted exposition on the dangers of intellectual property theft and corporate malfeasance, and a warning to copyright all handouts. Whispering to Maggie, Janet can't help but surreptitiously eye the orator. She turns around and sees two teachers knitting, one dozing off, and another lying in fetal position atop a table.

Looking forward in disbelief, Janet tries to refocus. She's staring at the screen overhead when to her surprise she's struck with the sudden urge to ask a question herself—it appears their IT guy has been left off the committee.

The week prior, between reliving college football highlights, he suggests to Janet this might happen but Janet is incredulous until now. Why on earth would you exclude your resident technology specialist from the committee overseeing technology?

She's on the precipice of falling into a timeless trap. In staff meetings there are two options: engage with the subject or relax, let it float by. You can either check out or weigh in. If you feel strongly enough, like Janet seems to about the technology committee and like several teachers clearly do about discipline and attendance, it can be difficult to remain silent.

Though you might want to consider the occasion. You might realize it's more effective to raise your concern with administrators directly, with those in a position to do something about it, in an alternate setting; you might talk to them in person instead of replying to all, for which your colleagues might thank you.

Except in that case, other teachers won't hear your opinion and they might agree your IT guy is, in fact, being marginalized and that, in any sane world, he ought to be included on the technology committee. But as older and wiser teachers are often fond of saying, if you try to make sense of it all, it will drive you crazy. So Janet keeps her hands in her lap. She lets it drift past. She doesn't take the bait.

She does, however, start singing happy birthday. When her friend and department chair Reuben stands to notify the staff of Wednesday's upcoming catered lunch—a rarity in education (in this case Chinese chicken salad)—Janet strikes up the tune and smiles at Maggie. Maggie chimes in as well and soon the entire faculty is crooning arrhythmically. Reuben is embarrassed and though they have already serenaded him at lunch over a buttercream birthday cake, this rendition is the icing. Great work, staff. Next topic.

An assistant principal then introduces a gentleman wearing wire-rim glasses and a blue polo shirt tucked into black jeans, his long hair silver and thinning. She says he's here to talk about the copy machines. The gentleman is a passionate advocate for copy machine maintenance and procedure and though he's motivational, his appearance is also distracting. Janet hears him say, "Confession: the marijuana I smoked at Woodstock would be considered bunk by kids today." Then the group text messages start rolling in.

"Wasn't this guy in *A Christmas Carol*?" someone writes beneath an image of Ebenezer Scrooge. Janet receives a picture of a drifter throwing a peace sign, a Nick Nolte booking photo, a portrait of Benjamin Franklin, a poster of David Carradine in *Kung Fu*. Looking up from her phone Janet sees a handful of grinning, faintly illuminated faces.

All of which makes one question why teachers are so much like their students. Maybe it's because they've worked in schools for so long they've forgotten what the real world is actually like. Teachers spend most of their professional lives engulfed in a sea of adolescence, emerging for brief moments like break, lunch, and staff meetings to visit with other adults, so a measure of juvenile acculturation is bound to occur.

Nevertheless, if this were a classroom most teachers would be offended by their faculty's behavior. Realizing she's equally at fault, Janet tucks her phone into her pocket and feigns attention. When the gentleman is finished they applaud and he leaves the room. Then their principal stands to wrap things up. She reminds staff to affix parking decals to their rear windows and requests they don't occupy disabled spots even though those spaces are closest to the classrooms. Ending on a positive note, the principal's secretary conducts a raffle for items donated by a friendly parent.

"And the winner is . . . 3-7-9-3-7-0."

"So close!" Janet calls out, elbowing Maggie in the ribs.

Finally, it's time to go. The principal dismisses the room but as she does a math teacher flies down the center aisle waiving his arms to get everyone's attention. It appears one bullet on the agenda has been overlooked. The math teacher asks those who haven't posed for their yearbook photos to stand against the back wall where a makeshift booth has been erected. Janet can't remember if her picture has already been taken but seeing a line quickly form she walks out with Maggie instead.

"Why do we even meet?" Maggie asks after leaving the conference room. "That was one giant memo." Janet doesn't have a good answer. It seems much of the previous hour's information could have been conveyed electronically.

But then again not all teachers read their email and many carp about not being informed so sometimes it's necessary to convey important messages, those you don't want overlooked, in person. Assembling to explain critical announcements may well be necessary, though question-and-answer sessions designed to clarify often morph into full-throated deliberation, which becomes prohibitively difficult with a ninety-person staff.

Of course there are other reasons to meet. Since teachers barely see one another, each the king of their lonely castle, it's useful to chat with members of other departments, hear what various teachers are planning, learn about interesting activities going on at school. These informal exchanges can pay big dividends provided they aren't stifled by excessively regulated conversation protocols, and especially when accompanied by food. After all, an effective faculty is a united one, and a united faculty is well fed.

Also since meeting time is limited—many districts contractually mandate just one hour per week outside the regular schedule—the time teachers spend in staff meetings detracts from their time to collaborate with other teachers in small groups. So if you're going to bring everyone together it's important to be clear about the objectives. Activities fostering cohesion and bonhomie, such as eating, seem like time well spent. Perhaps a quick dissemination of

the most important information. Maybe some micro-professional development, a few teaching tips to bring home along with those leftover cookies.
Anything else may not be worth the effort.

"I don't know," Janet replies to Maggie as they walk away.

"These staff infections are always so painful," Maggie adds, visibly shaken
by the ordeal.

Janet shrugs. She wishes she could offer her a cure.

KEY IDEAS

- At staff meetings, teachers often behave like their students.
- Staff meetings should exist to explain and clarify important information,
  provide useful professional development, and enhance camaraderie among
  the faculty (i.e., eating).

Chapter 35

Never Chaperone a High School Dance

During Noah's first year of teaching he's asked, ever so kindly, to chaperone prom. Though not terribly excited about the prospect of watching teenagers bump and grind—after all, he's not so far removed from the experience himself—he very much wants to be retained in the district and knows enough to say yes to anything, including this.

Riding public transportation, Noah walks the last quarter mile to the pier where teachers, administrators, and leadership students are making final preparations by the boat. It seems the high school's junior-senior prom will be held on a chartered ferry in the bay.

Noah is assigned to taking tickets and manning the entrance. Soon students begin to arrive and things are going smoothly until several girls approach in shiny pastel dresses.

"Oh hey!" they yell, and lean in for a hug.

"Hey. Hi," he responds awkwardly, arms flat against his body like a sentry from Buckingham Palace. *Loosen up, you're a teacher now*, he tells himself, but Noah still can't believe he's attending another prom.

When everyone has boarded, the ferry undocks from the pier. Noah is standing along the stern railing with a handful of others taking in the dying light. As they putter into the bay, the sun meets the horizon beneath an aging bridge in the middle distance, casting an amber glow against wispy western clouds. The water is calm, the scene almost peaceful.

When stars emerge, piercing the darkening sky, Noah walks inside feeling refreshed. Teenagers mill about a linoleum dance floor drinking Shirley Temples and other bright syrupy drinks. He climbs the stairs and encounters an ersatz gambling parlor replete with blackjack, poker, and roulette. Tables are brimming with students making wild if purely sentimental bets while adults disseminate stacks of plastic chips.

Weaving through the bustle, Noah feels a tug at his jacket sleeve from a teacher signaling her readiness for a break, so he sits behind the curving green felt, tidies the chip tray, and begins flipping cards. Occupying third base is a reckless if charismatic adolescent who hits a soft seventeen. Nonetheless his prudence pays off.

"Too many. Dealer busts!" Noah calls out to a round of cheers.

After nearly an hour, he's beginning to get hungry when word spreads it's time to eat. Though a buffet line has formed downstairs, the senior class advisor, a social studies teacher, ushers Noah and several others to the top deck where a small room has been arranged for staff. There they enjoy a relaxing dinner of chicken piccata and steamed vegetables. Just as Noah is beginning to think his apprehension over the evening is overblown, however, he notices a heavy bass-thump emanating from below. Eventually everyone rises, in a manner he will recognize years later as preparing for battle, and fashions their sternest of expressions.

"Guess it's time to go downstairs," says the class advisor.

The teachers spill onto a scene of unadulterated horror. Somehow in the short space of a meal the buffet area has become a shadowy strobe-lit dance hall, an underbelly of adolescent gluttony and lust one might reasonably mistake for some juvenile incarnation of the outer rings of the Nine Circles of Hell.

The once-empty linoleum parquet is now pumping with throngs of teen-agers gyrating, shaking, smushing against one another in a humid mass of hysteria. Following the others' lead Noah encircles the pit, not exactly sure what he's supposed to be doing. Then he sees a teacher dive in, threading her way deep into the inner sanctum of the mob to separate several swaying, covalently linked pelvises.

"Break it up, guys," she demands, cleaving her arms through transgressing folds of silk and polyester.

Noah feels light-headed. He's not prepared for this. He takes a seat next to an empty window, attempting to regroup and unsure of his next move, when a cool droplet strikes the back of his neck. Instinctively he looks up and notices beads of water forming on white weathered beams overhead. Behind him the windows are thick with condensation, some beginning to streak like a wineglass. The air smells of exuberance and musk.

Noah leaps to his feet, frightened by the music, the moisture, the swarm of adolescents raging beneath syncopated electric lights, and hurries upstairs in defeat. He doesn't want to be there; he doesn't want to see what he has seen. Reentering the poker room he finds another teacher dealing Texas Hold 'Em to a sparsely populated table of boys who for one reason or another don't want to dance.

"You okay there?" the teacher asks.

"Uh-huh."

Noah feels dazed, shaken like a motorist who has just witnessed a grisly accident.

"Oh you've been downstairs," the teacher says. "That's a mistake. Better stay up here with me."

And so he does. For the remainder of the evening Noah alternates between dealing cards and meandering on the deck, taking in the crisp wind and the ambient lights of the bay. It will all be over soon.

That night Noah learns a lesson. He tells himself he'll never chaperone another dance—which is a lie, of course, but a lie he needs to believe at the time. The thing is teachers have to chaperone *something*. As part of their jobs they're contractually required to oversee extracurricular activities. In some districts, for example, each teacher must earn one hundred supervision points per year. Fortunately, there are many options apart from muggy discos on the lower deck of a ship.

Usually teachers select supervision assignments in mid-August. At the anointed hour, say 8:00 on a Monday morning, you simply register online through an in-house database. But be sure you have chosen in advance because openings are filled on a first-come, first-served basis and the most desirable selections will be snagged by 8:15, in which case you'll find yourself, once again, chaperoning a dance.

And if you feel uncomfortable telling teenagers to stop freaking and separate their torsos, if you'd rather not admonish high-school boys for approaching girls from behind, or high-school girls for putting their hands on the floor and their posteriors in the sky, then blowing the registration is not something you'll want to do. So you better have a game plan, and you better sign up on time.

Of the more desirable alternatives, one can also supervise sporting events, concerts, or graduation, or serve as a class advisor or coach. Though the choir's spring and holiday performances are charming, and while you may participate in but not technically work graduation, you might prefer supervising football and basketball games since they are fairly relaxed, often entertaining, and occasionally the source of great excitement. Like the Saturday afternoon several months later when Noah's assistant principal chases down a streaker at homecoming.

Evidently, a member of the track team has decided it will be wise to dash from one end of the grounds to the other wearing only a lucha libre mask and running shoes. While the cheerleaders are readying for their halftime performance, he materializes from the northern end of the track already in full sprint. But little does he know Noah's assistant principal was formerly a defensive back in the Canadian Football League.

Trailing by a good twenty yards, the AP takes off after him. As they cross midfield, racing down the track in full view of the crowded stands, the defensive back begins to gain ground. By the time the streaker reaches the southern end of the field the AP is directly on his heels, and when the streaker attempts to scale the chain-link fence the AP yanks him down, denuding the delinquent of his disguise, and a good portion of his dignity.

To this day, a near-perfect photograph taken by a secretary in the stands remains: the streaker is approaching the fifty-yard line, privates miraculously shielded by the head of an onlooking fan, while in the left-hand third of the frame the defensive back-turned-administrator is immortalized mid-stride, arms bent and legs kicking, on his way to executing one of the great tackles in school history.

Clearly this much excitement is anomalous. While one cannot hope for similar drama at each supervision, one can at least avoid several common pitfalls. Accumulating one hundred points isn't that big of a deal; you see a few games, listen to a few concerts, schedule a handful of club meetings. These things are all integral if extracurricular components of a school, and since students must be overseen at school-related events, teachers need to help out. It shouldn't all fall on the shoulders of administrators and campus supervisors—even if they played professional football and can track down the fleetest of naked sprinters.

In the end, no matter what else you do, whatever supervision assignments you may choose, just make sure you sign up as soon as possible. Because like Noah you do not want to get stuck chaperoning a high-school dance. Seriously, you will regret it.

KEY IDEAS

- Extracurricular student activities require teacher supervision.
- Teachers have many options to choose from, including sporting events and dances, though the latter can offer a uniquely unpleasant experience.

Chapter 36

How Do You Say "Teacher" in French?

For the first time in Devin's teaching career, a group of students has risen in unison as he enters the room. Except these are not Devin's students, and this is not his country.

He's sitting in the classroom of a public school in Orthez, France, located in the heart of Basque country near the southwest border with Spain, a land of unmatched physical beauty where, like now in early spring, the snowcapped Pyrenees feed a web of sinuous tributaries, the whirling air of the Atlantic summons, and everywhere the hills are a verdant green. But this classroom is stark. There are no pictures on the walls, no color, and no clock. The teacher is standing above his students on a raised platform lecturing about European geography.

The students stand as Devin enters.

"*Bonjour*," he says inelegantly, then finds a corner seat toward the back.

Devin has been told the teacher knows he's stopping by. Traveling with a group of students from his own public high school located miles from the coast of another ocean, he's there with Monsieur Fred, the trip leader and French language teacher who created this exchange some twenty years prior, and Alexa, a school counselor.

Students from Orthez visited in late October and now they're in France on the second leg of the adventure. Last fall Devin taught the Frenchies how to play baseball and sing "Take Me Out to the Ball Game"—cornerstones of American culture and a requirement when their team was on the cusp of winning another World Series. Now he's wondering what the Frenchies will teach him.

In some ways, this classroom thousands of miles from his own appears very much the same. There are whiteboards, pencil sharpeners and tissues, rows of desks facing a teacher at the front of the room. But the largest difference, other than an elevated stage and walls inordinately devoid of character, is the students. Most exhibit a blasé countenance, a laissez-faire affect bordering on outright ennui. A majority of students near Devin are not listening at all; they're talking among themselves oblivious to the ministrations of their instructor, acting as if the class is unimportant. Which, Devin will later learn, it might be.

To be honest, he's judging. The teacher seems knowledgeable and well versed but Devin is surprised by the teacher's relationship with his students. It's like there are two different worlds occupying the same physical space: the teacher lectures, impervious to distractions, while pockets of students converse as if at break or on lunch.

Before class ends Devin sneaks out to visit the lounge. There teachers are grading papers, lesson planning, and sipping cafés, all dressed in what appears to be the universal uniform of the profession: just nice enough, with a nod to comfort over style, and accentuated with teacher-armor like elbow patches, buttons, and big jewelry. It is a scene both comforting and familiar.

When the period is finished Devin heads to the cafeteria to meet Monsieur Fred, Alexa, the *proviseur*, and his vice *proviseur* for lunch prepared by the school chef. The chef emerges to greet them in his traditional whites then returns to the kitchen. They enjoy an hors d'oeuvre, a salad, an entrée, and a cheese course, all accompanied by bottles of red and white wine. They're eating and drinking and somehow Devin has learned to speak flawless French. When dessert arrives the vice *proviseur* pulls a bottle of Calvados from his back office. *Now this is how one teaches afternoon classes*, Devin muses. The possibilities seem endless.

After the meal, Devin, Monsieur Fred, and Alexa thank their hosts profusely and then walk down the hill into town. In the afternoon, they return to school and meet up with their students whom they have not seen since leaving them with host families for the long weekend. Separated from their teachers and classmates for several days, they have been wholly immersed in French culture.

Some stay afloat while others drown, fish out of water in an unfamiliar sea. Soon they will return to Paris but this weekend is the true apex of their trip. Debriefing in an empty conference room, students tell stories of helplessness and humiliation, of struggling to find the right phrases for "I'm full," "The shower is cold," and "I have wet feet." They talk about successfully communicating across the linguistic divide, about the liberation that comes with letting go and giving in.

"Last night I dreamt in French!" a student exclaims.

Devin mentions the benefits of the Learn by Embarrassment method of language acquisition and says there are fewer ways to grow as quickly than being corrected by a local after making a mistake. He applauds students for stepping outside their comfort zones and onto unfamiliar terrain.

This, here, is the real power of exchange programs, the apotheosis of authentic learning. What better way to master the basics of French than to practice with its native speakers? What better place to apply what one learns in the classroom than out in the world? In the same way it's said meditating for one minute at the Tiger's Nest, a Buddhist monastery in the Himalayas, is equivalent to three months of regular meditation elsewhere, the same is true of cultural exchange: one minute of conversation abroad is equivalent to months of traditional instruction at home. Even if that's an exaggeration it's not by much.

Afterward, students rejoin their Frenchies in class and Monsieur Fred, Alexa, and Devin leave the school. Upon exiting, they notice several clusters of teenagers loitering beside the front gate smoking cigarettes and flicking their used butts to the ground. On the drive to their hotel in Saint-Jean-de-Luz, an idyllic fishing village turned tourist resort where Louis XIV once married Maria Theresa of Spain, they discuss the day's events.

Or more like Monsieur Fred talks while Devin and Alexa listen. Devin gazes out the window at herds of white cattle roaming emerald hills, past road signs with exotic names like Salies-de-Bearn, Bellocq, and Espellete, and off toward the Pyrenees in the distance. Monsieur Fred explains the French school system revolves around the baccalaureate, so grades are less important and therefore students don't listen as closely during class or stress as often until preparing for the high-stakes final exam.

Monsieur Fred also tells them students attend school for more hours each day but also take longer breaks throughout. One interesting result of this extended schedule means the revered notion of the "student-athlete" is a foreign concept in France. There are no school-affiliated sports teams and no crosstown rivalries, traditions so intricately woven into the fabric of American life that it's nearly impossible to imagine anything different.

Instead, from a relatively young age children are placed into schools emphasizing either athletics or academics, experiencing but a taste of the other. Devin says if one admires the student-athlete ideal, believes in the ancient notion of *mens sana in corpore sano*—a sound mind in a sound body—one may be troubled that French adolescents have to choose either school or sports, that they cannot pursue both as ardently as in America. Perhaps this is because the French are more concerned with thinking, Monsieur Fred opines.

Monsieur Fred recalls the French ethic of "*égalité*," social and political equality, and says it's manifested in areas like education and medicine. He recounts a youthful experience traveling in Marseille and hoping to visit the doctor for a laceration that may or may not require stitches. Having no medical insurance Monsieur Fred is sent away with bandages, balm, and a bottle of pills but no exorbitant medical bill—a concept as foreign to Americans as student-athletes to the French.

Monsieur Fred also informs Devin that quickly joining a desirable district like theirs would never happen in France. He says French teachers are assigned nationally, similar to the army, with most rookies placed in less attractive areas—to put it tactfully—like near Brittany in the north. Given America's struggling schools filled with young teachers, he adds it's worth considering how both systems can incentivize career professionals to work in underserved areas with the neediest students.

They pull onto the narrow streets of Saint-Jean-de-Luz with an afternoon free to themselves, and enough sunlight overhead to traverse the cobblestone alleys, take in the salty air, and contemplate their next meal, to nearly forget they're working. They won't see students again until the following morning; and in several days they'll depart for Paris where, having already checked off obligatory visits to the Notre Dame, Eiffel Tower, and Louvre, they'll explore lesser-known delights like Berthillion ice cream on the Île Saint-Louis, falafel in the Marais, and the open markets of Rue Mouffetard.

They'll enter the Place des Vosges for an impromptu *sieste* in the grassy square, and upon leaving they'll encounter a group of students at a corner café eating pastries, one with an illicit glass of wine. In that moment they'll remember they're chaperones, that they're not merely hunting for the city's best crepes and coziest bistros, and they'll call the student's parents to inform them she has broken the rules and will be suspended upon her return.

But back in St.-Jean the day is theirs. The students are nowhere in sight. And, after hiking along cliffs above an iridescent cove, they agree bouillabaisse sounds like just the right choice for dinner.

KEY IDEAS

- Student exchange programs exemplify authentic learning.
- Chaperoning such trips is deeply enjoyable and illuminating, but it's still work.

Chapter 37

Of Unions, Cows, and Cheese

Chris is staring at a half-empty jar of queso, contemplating tucking into another spoonful of artificial goodness. Below him four or five strawberry tops, pistachio detritus, and a pile of tortilla chips are all that remain on his paper plate. *You've consumed most of that queso already*, he thinks to himself, *better leave the rest alone.*

But the jar lies within arm's reach, practically under his nose, and he can detect its strangely pleasant off-gassing redolent of Little League nachos, summertime, and fun.

Actually, it'd be a shame to squander perfectly good tortilla chips, he rationalizes, *and plus Candice gets it just for you. She* wants *you to eat it. Don't be impolite.*

Self-discipline exhausted, Chris scoops a large dollop of queso onto his leftover chips, then mentally reenters the conversation. Sitting in a conference room late one afternoon at an alternative high school in his district, Chris has drifted from a discussion about agency fees with the executive board of his teachers' union.

The agency fee discussion, the last item on the agenda, is meandering. As a president in charge of facilitating meetings, Chris is shamelessly seeking refuge in a foodlike substance that the treasurer Candice customarily purchases on his behalf. *Just get to the point already*, says the impatient and less-diplomatic voice inside Chris's head.

"It's ridiculous we don't require teachers to be in the union."

"I think forcing teachers to join will only worsen the problem we're trying to solve."

"Well it's unfair paying dues while freeloaders keep more of their paychecks every month and still get the raises and benefits we negotiate."

"But we can't just demand everyone becomes a member. That's not fair either."

Finally, the heart of the issue. In some states, like California, unions are allowed to charge nonmembers an "agency fee" to offset the cost of activities like bargaining for better conditions and compensation. If nonmembers object to this fee, they can pay an equivalent sum to a philanthropy instead. But Chris's union doesn't impose agency fees at all.

Nonmembers keep the extra one percent of their salaries—that would ordinarily go to the union or a charity—while still enjoying the same perks, like raises and class size reductions, as everyone else. On one hand, compelling teachers to join the union doesn't feel right, but on the other, it seems inequitable that those same people nonetheless enjoy the fruits of their union's labor.

"Must we decide right now?" says vice president Tina from across the table. "We've already worked through most of the agenda and it's getting kind of late."

The group nods in agreement. This afternoon they've already voted to hire a note taker for school board meetings, clarified contract language around personal necessity versus sick leave, finalized a date for the next social event, and listened to updates about counselor caseloads, access to personnel files, and the union newsletter.

In other meetings, they consider equally banal items like student attendance, staff development, and the school year calendar, the sorts of ground-level activities that are a union's bread-and-butter, local, personal, apolitical. Mainly a union's job is to uphold the contract—the "collective bargaining agreement"—and to solve problems, to help resolve conflicts between teachers and the administration so that schools function as smoothly as possible with the least amount of friction.

Shifting to an agency fee model is a significant decision and a potentially divisive one. It's something Chris's executive board, comprised of teachers and counselors elected from across the district, wants to get right, to ensure is reflective of the will of their faculty.

"How about this," Chris suggests through a mostly-empty mouth. "Why don't we hear what teachers have to say during our next site visits. Let's get a read and see where everyone's at."

Thankfully, except for two site reps who want to institute agency fees straightaway, nearly everyone agrees. Over the next month, Chris will visit a different high school each week, meeting with and listening to staff, gauging the collective mood across his district. He'll encounter one school rather indifferent to the idea, another fairly against, and a third sharply divided between those happy with the status quo and others ready for revolution.

In addition to installing agency fees, this later group is also agitating for more active steps such as administering a "satisfaction survey," implementing administrator evaluations, even showing up en masse to school board meetings to make their opinions heard. But Chris will also encounter many teachers who don't want the union at the tip of the spear, instead preferring it takes a more behind-the-scenes role nudging the district in the right direction.

"Great," Chris says, hoping to conclude what's been an unusually long meeting. "Anything else?" Around the table members of the executive board shake their heads. "Sounds good—"

"Well, there is one more thing I'd like to bring up," says a vocal site rep as several teachers shift in their seats. He begins talking about student-to-teacher ratios but Chris is once again in the process of checking out. He gazes across the room at sunlight knifing through the window, illuminating tendrils of coiling dust and a now-mostly empty jar of processed cheese. He contemplates polishing it off.

The site rep is saying words like "Cap" and "Size" and "Department" and "Average," but Chris's mind is drifting. Staring out the window, he thinks about the nature of unions, about why they've become so politicized, and about how he got here in the first place. Two years ago, Chris joined the negotiating team because he considered unions a force for good, a necessary component in a healthy democracy (though equally fallible and prone to corruption, much like democracies themselves).

Chris also looked up to several retired teachers who not only inspired him in his own career but also helped establish their union as one of the first in the state. He wanted to contribute like those before him so he got involved. Who knew he'd also get free queso. Talk about perks.

Yet Chris's view seems in contradiction with public opinion. Even though unions have helped bolster the middle class, diminish inequality, and give rise to the weekend, they still suffer in the popular psyche, and teachers unions most of all. Despite unions existing for firefighters, nurses, actors, journalists, pilots, police, musicians, athletes, engineers, and more, some still believe unions function to insulate bad teachers, to make sure no one gets fired. It's doubtful these same people hold similar beliefs about so many other union-supported professions.

Ideally, unions should exist to ensure their members work under the best possible conditions for the best possible salary—but also to make the system more fair, not less. And when they devolve into protecting the interests of their members above all else, above those of the people they serve, like students, then unions should be reformed.

But what happens when mothers must exhaust all their sick days before taking maternity leave, or same-sex partners are barred from receiving the benefits of a spouse? Who will advocate for those who have been treated unfairly? What is to be done when forty students are placed in a classroom instead of the contractual thirty-three, or a teacher is accused of impropriety by one of her students? Who will ensure a just system of resolving disputes? Surely not each teacher alone. Instead of everyone for themselves, why not all for one? Why not elect representatives to speak for the faculty at large? Why *not* a teachers union?

As the site rep finishes his peroration, Chris scrutinizes the remaining dip at the bottom of the jar but decides to abstain. A measure of temperance is in order, he convinces himself, and plus it's time to go.

"All right, let's leave it there. Thanks, everyone, for coming," he says, "and thanks to Candice for hosting and bringing the food."

They stand up to leave.

"You'd better finish that," Candice adds with a goading smile.

Outside, the campus has long since emptied out. Chris exits the conference room alongside vice president Tina, walking through a small courtyard with chalk-scrawled blacktop and potted flowers. He leaves feeling good about the executive board's efforts to improve the lives of teachers—not only for their own sake but also for those they serve, enhancing the opportunities of those they're educating. Because like cows and cheese, as they say in California, happy teachers make happy students.

Perhaps this has been a teachers union's true purpose all along.

KEY IDEA

• Teachers' unions serve an essential role in education, though they are neither infallible nor immune from reform.

Who Cares?

"Who cares?" I'll often ask my students during some unit of study. I'm trying to emphasize the relevance of what we're learning because students who are unable to find value in a subject are less likely to be invested in it, and therefore more likely to forget. Empty facts, as I'm sure you'll recall from many a high-school lecture, go in one ear and out the other.

So "Who cares?" I say, opting for an informal and hopefully engaging way of asking students why the French Revolution, Fourth Amendment, or Federal Reserve matters, why it's significant, why they should stop, take notice, and remember. Sometimes posing the question more directly is effective too. "How will this make a difference in your lives a month, a year or even ten years from now?" you might ask.

Though let's hope you receive a satisfying answer, indeed any answer at all. If not, the silence will be deafening. You'll feel like the last three weeks you've spent teaching students about the causes and effects of the Industrial Revolution have been for nothing. Sure they may be able to recall the architect of the seed drill, the purpose of the flying shuttle, or the efficiency of the spinning jenny, but if students can't place these disruptive technological inventions in their historical context, articulate why they resonate today, or explain what they might imply for their lives in this century, then what you've taught is for naught. You haven't done your job.

The same holds true for this collection of essays. Yes, I hope you've learned what it's like to be a teacher. I hope you can see we're not all saints or slouches, heroes or zeros, and that at the end of the school day we're real people. I hope you better understand the importance of classroom management; the various ways of structuring a lesson; the many considerations when assigning homework and determining final grades; the value of showing movies in class; the inconvenience of getting a sub; the demands of reaching all students in a room of mixed backgrounds and abilities.

I hope you appreciate the dilemma of being either feared or loved in the classroom; the chances for embarrassment when improvising in front of a class; the similarities of teaching to coaching; the perverse implications of the golden handcuffs; the essential function of teachers unions; the joy in learning you have helped a student when you least expect it; the sensation of a heart at once full and broken for a kid who is trying his hardest to succeed in spite of every obstacle standing in his way.

I hope you realize the discipline it takes to refrain from making fun of students who say silly things or wear amusing clothes; the dismay of chaperoning a high-school dance; the benefits of cultural exchange programs; the darker moments of insecurity about your teaching abilities; the significance of a mentor teacher when you're new to the classroom; the fundamental necessity of lunchtime with colleagues; the mild discomfort of not using the bathroom for extended periods of time; the irritation in hearing "good for you" for becoming a teacher.

And I hope you can picture the ritualized dog-and-pony shows that are Back to School Night and Open House; the timelessness of pep rallies; the banality of staff development; the ecstasy of year-end teacher parties; and the sheer terror of waking up from a nightmare in which you are naked and late for class.

But if greater understanding is your only takeaway, I don't think this will be enough. Who cares? Why does it matter? And what comes next? If you're a student—and it's only now dawning on me that students may actually read these pages—perhaps you'll have more empathy for your teachers; you might think about the many factors we consider when making decisions, and thus treat us extra well, or at least criticize us extra thoughtfully. If you're a parent, same.

If you're a voter, a leader, or anyone with the ability to influence public debate, I would hope you consider the policy implications of these essays. As I write in "Happy Hour," the teaching profession suffers from a lack of reverence. And if teaching doesn't rise to the level of esteem generally held for doctors, lawyers, and businesspeople, then I believe it should.

If we enhance teachers' compensation and allow them the freedom to practice according to their sense of professional standards, as we do in medicine and in law, and if we make the job more competitive by raising the bar and the barriers to entry, people will truly begin to value what we do. More graduates will want to become teachers both because they can make a decent salary and because their friends and family, even attractive singles at the bar, will admire the profession they have chosen. "Damn, it's not easy to become a teacher," they will think. "That person must be smart, and they must make pretty good money too."

Furthermore, if we remodel staff and professional development so both are more useful we will keep more career teachers in the classroom. Adopting lesson study, or *jugyō kenkyū* as it's known in Japan, in which teachers collaborate to design a lesson, observe the lesson being taught, then debrief the lesson's efficacy, will help teachers hone their craft. Like medical rounds, instructional rounds in education would also be highly informative. In many ways, teachers are kings and queens of their lonely castles and bringing other adults into the room is a much-needed advancement (though also discomfiting after so many years on one's own). Unfortunately, both lesson study and instructional rounds bump up against the well-proven statistic that American educators teach for more hours and with less planning time than the rest of their global peers. It would be nice to have greater opportunity for career growth but hey—at least we're world leaders. In short, as I conclude in "Of Cows, Unions, and Cheese," happy teachers make happy students. Well-respected, well-compensated, well-developed teachers will produce well-rounded, well-educated young adults.

Finally, if you're a teacher I hope I've represented our profession fairly, in a way you might yourself. You know how great a career this is and how great it can be. You know that once you've been infected with the teaching bug there is no cure.

You may be traveling over the summer and stumble upon a curious artifact or meet an interesting person and dream up a great activity for the fall. You might be reading the newspaper over winter break and find the perfect article for an upcoming unit. Or you might be showering before school and devise an entirely new plan for your eight o'clock lesson. It's a lifelong affliction; some might say obsession.

For everyone, I have wanted to add my perspective to the larger narrative surrounding teaching because I think a fuller, more forthright accounting of what we do will make for more effective teachers, more able students, and ultimately a more enlightened society. In the end, I'd like to leave you with this: I love to teach. I hope you will help propel this profession forward because it can be a calling, a great career more people should experience—not only by sitting in a desk, but also standing above it.

About the Author

Aaron Pribble is the author of *Pitching in the Promised Land: A Story of the First and Only Season in the Israel Baseball League* (2011). An award-winning educator whose work includes *"Pribble is a Chiller": Student Input and Teacher Evaluations, Dreaming of Baseball in Havana,* and *Fastball in the Desert* among other publications, Aaron teaches social studies at Tamalpais High School in Mill Valley, California.